Life Under the Shadow of the Almighty

Life Under the Shadow of the Almighty

A Journey Through Psalm 91

LANDIS BROWN

Foreword by John Nicholas

WIPF & STOCK · Eugene, Oregon

LIFE UNDER THE SHADOW OF THE ALMIGHTY
A Journey Through Psalm 91

Copyright © 2025 Landis Brown. All rights reserved. Except for brief quotations in critical publications or reviews, no part of this book may be reproduced in any manner without prior written permission from the publisher. Write: Permissions, Wipf and Stock Publishers, 199 W. 8th Ave., Suite 3, Eugene, OR 97401.

Wipf & Stock
An Imprint of Wipf and Stock Publishers
199 W. 8th Ave., Suite 3
Eugene, OR 97401

www.wipfandstock.com

PAPERBACK ISBN: 979-8-3852-4437-9
HARDCOVER ISBN: 979-8-3852-4438-6
EBOOK ISBN: 979-8-3852-4439-3

VERSION NUMBER 041725

Unless otherwise noted, Scripture quotations are taken from The Authorized (King James) Version. Rights in the Authorized Version in the United Kingdom are vested in the Crown. Reproduced by permission of the Crown's patentee, Cambridge University Press.

Scripture quotations marked ESV are from The Holy Bible, English Standard Version (ESV), Text Edition 2016, copyright © 2001 by Crossway Bible, a publishing ministry of Good News Publishers. All Rights Reserved

Scripture quotations marked NASB are from the New American Standard Bible®, Copyright © 1960, 1962, 1963, 1968, 1971, 1972, 1973, 1975, 1977, 1995 by The Lockman Foundation. All rights reserved.

To my beloved wife, Faith,
whose mercy and grace reflect Christ's love daily.
Your unwavering support and kindness sustain me more than words can express.

To my children, Eva, Duncan, and Knox,
whose joy, curiosity, and steadfast love are a constant light in my life.
You encourage, inspire, and remind me why I press forward.

Contents

Foreword by John Nicholas | ix
Preface | xi

1. **A Shadow of Rest** | 1
   Psalm 91:1

2. **A Shadow of Deliverance** | 15
   Psalm 91:2–3

3. **A Life Lived Under God's Protection** | 28
   Psalm 51:4

4. **A Life Lived in the Absence of Fear** | 43
   Psalm 91:5–10

5. **A Life Preserved** | 62
   Psalm 91:11–13

6. **A Life Marked by Longevity** | 82
   Psalm 91:14–16

Bibliography | 101

Foreword

When reading *Life Under the Shadow of the Almighty: A Journey Through Psalm 91*, I could not help but recall a story from my father's time in the Navy. In the 1950s, he served as an enlisted sailor aboard the USS *Uhlman* (DD-687), a destroyer caught in a relentless typhoon in the South China Sea for four or five days. He described the towering, violent waves—so immense that when the 375-foot-long ship crested one and plunged into the next, the propellers would spin in open air. At times, the vessel crashed into the cavernous troughs below, teetering on the edge of breaking apart, much like Jonah's ship in Jonah 1:4.

Landis's reflection about abiding and finding shelter in the Lord, drawn from Ps 91, brought this scene vividly to mind. For my father and his shipmates, there was no refuge—nowhere to run, nowhere to hide, only the storm. With no escape, they could do nothing but endure—minute by minute, hour by hour, day after day. Nevertheless, as I read Landis's exposition of Ps 91, I was reminded that we are never truly without shelter in life's fiercest trials. In Christ, we have a refuge here and now—our shelter in the tempest, our stronghold until we reach those heavenly shores.

This book is more than an exposition; it is a careful and faithful handling of Ps 91, rich in both exegetical depth and practical application. Having known Landis for years—through postgraduate studies, pastoral ministry, and, most importantly, personal friendship—I can attest to his deep love for the church and his unwavering commitment to the inerrant, infallible word of God.

Foreword

His pastoral heart is evident on every page as he points readers to the only true Savior, Jesus Christ.

It is my joy to commend this book to all who long for a deeper understanding of Ps 91 and the unwavering refuge found in our great Triune God.

John Nicholas, DMin
Senior Pastor
Grace Reformed Church

Preface

PSALM 91 PAINTS YAHWEH as a fortress for the saints, a refuge from the storm, and a shelter from the tempest. Charles Spurgeon claims that Ps 91 is a "balm for wounded spirits and a cordial for fainting souls."[1] If there ever was a psalm that paints the God of heaven as a place of refuge, a sanctuary, a bulwark, a shelter, as the source of all comfort, all provision, all protection, and all rest, it is Ps 91. From its onset, God's sovereignty over the afflicted is introduced in the two names of God in v. 1, namely, "the Most High" and "the Almighty." As the Most High, no one can offer greater comfort and rest than this God, and, as the Almighty, there is no one above this God; therefore, his shadow alone provides unmatched benefits for those who abide in him. Thus, there is no place of refuge that is more peaceful and no place of deliverance that is more guaranteed than under the shadow of this God, whom Moses calls both "the Most High" and "the Almighty."

While v. 1 provides some universal names for Yahweh, Moses in v. 2 nails down even further which God he is speaking of that believers should abide in if they want to be found under his shadow. In v. 2, Moses begins to use some names that he has personally given God, describing who God is to him. Moses calls him "my refuge and my fortress: my God; in him will I trust," validating even more that there is no other whose shadow alone can provide the rest and comfort offered under his shadow. In vv. 2–4, Moses shows not only that rest is offered within the shadow of God but

---

1. Spurgeon, *Treasury of David*, 91.

also deliverance. Moses switches to the third person singular in v. 3 to say that it is "he," the Most High, the Almighty, Yahweh alone who delivers, thus giving another promise to those who continually abide under the shadow of the Almighty, namely, that "he" will deliver them. Under Yahweh's shadow, these will find deliverance from the greatest threats that may revolt against him. For example, v. 3 shows shows two of the greatest threats to God's people, that God will deliver them from, namely the "snare of the fowler, and from the noisome pestilence. If Moses hasn't made life under the shadow of the Almighty seem sweet enough, in v. 4, he continues to take the reader on a tour to another place under God's shadow, specifically, a place of protection. Moses shows the reader in v. 4 that not only rest and deliverance are found under God's shadow but also protection. Moses shows the extent of Yahweh's protection, comparing him to a mother bird who covers her young with her pinions, providing a place of refuge under her wings. Through the imagery in v. 4, Moses shows that there is no safer place to be than under the shadow of the Almighty, where God pulls those who abide in him close, protecting them from the enemy.

Verse 5 introduces another promise tucked away between two indicative statements regarding those who continually abide with God in both v. 1 and vv. 9–10. It is those who continually abide in the secret place of the Most High (v. 1) and who have made him their dwelling place (vv. 9–10) that will no longer be afraid (v. 5). Due to all that God provides for his people who abide under his shadow, it will be these only who will find themselves living a life absent of fear. Moses fleshes out what a life absent of fear looks like for those who abide in the shadow of the Almighty in vv. 5b–8. Those who abide in God's shadow will not have to fear "the terror by night," etc., but only watch as God defeats their enemies, making them fall in countless numbers, according to vv. 7–8.

As this psalm progresses, Moses continues to take his readers on a guided tour through a life under the shadow of the Almighty, showing the reader the benefits to those who constantly abide with God. In vv. 11–13, Moses shows that God provides an extra layer of security to those who abide under his shadow, charging his angels to guard over those who are, according to vv. 1 and 9, abiding in him. Therefore, under the shadow of the Almighty, one will not only find rest, deliverance, and protection, but, according to vv. 11–13, Moses shows that God also preserves those who continually abide with him. In the latter verses of this psalm, Moses reinforces the entirety of the psalm by recording God's words affirming his promises of deliverance, protection, and so on to those who continually abide under his shadow, as alluded to by Moses. By taking his readers on a journey through life under the shadow of the Almighty, Moses reveals that there is no safer place, no more comforting and peaceful place to abide, than under the shadow of the Almighty. Like a child who finds comfort in his father's arms or a lamb who finds protection under their shepherd's staff, God's people will find true rest and peace from the enemy's schemes under the shadow of the Almighty. Like a shade tree that protects those who sit under it from the scorching heat, so does God's shadow provide those who abide under it a place of protection from the Evil One.

Psalm 91 brings comfort and solace to those who meditate on its truths. This psalm has brought comfort to those who have faced terminal illness, awaiting death to come. This psalm has encouraged those who have lost a loved one. Soldiers, amid battle, have raised the words of Ps 91 as a banner and waved its promises as a flag because it provided a resting place for them as they marched through the darkest times of their lives. For those in any battle, this psalm has pointed them to where they can find rest and comfort amid the war they are facing, namely under the shadow of the Almighty. The first verse alone has been called the 911 verse of all the Scripture. If one needs a quick reminder of the protecting and preserving power of God during times of trouble, one must turn to Ps 91:1. If one finds themselves living in fear, anxiety, and worry while facing the unknown, one must turn to Ps 91:1 to find rest and relief from their fear. If one finds oneself in spiritual warfare turmoil, unable to rest one's weary soul, one must turn to Ps 91:1 to be pointed to the One who provides the greatest of all rest, that is to say, the Most High. God's shadow alone, according to Moses, gives unmatched rest to those who continually abide in the secret place of the Most High.

If there ever was a man whose life was well spent abiding in the shadow of the Almighty, it was Moses. Many scholars attribute Moses as the writer of Ps 91 due to it following Ps 90, which explicitly states that it is a "Prayer of Moses."[2] Some ancient Jewish traditions, such as the Talmud, attribute Ps 91 to Moses. Also, the Midrash Tehillim supports this view, connecting it with Moses's authorship.[3] Psalm 91 is Moses's testimony of the rest and provision God provided him and Israel while leading them out of Egypt, through the Red Sea, and through the wilderness. Leading the children of Israel out of the bondage of the iron furnace of Egypt, through the Red Sea, through forty years of wilderness terrain, through the heat of the desert, and through one trial after another, Moses's longevity and survival was due to his abiding under the shadow of the Almighty. It will be Israel's liberation from Egypt and their sustaining in the desert that only comes through abiding under the shadow of the Almighty. While in Egypt, God alone will bring liberation to his people, striking Israel's enemies and leading them through the Red Sea out of Egypt on the dry ground; thus, God who is unchanging continues to do the same for those today who abide under his shadow.

God's shadow is a sweet spot for his people to live, providing a place of rest and protection from the harshest enemies. Under God's shadow, one simply needs to watch as the salvation of the Lord is manifest and God destroys the enemy of his people. Moses saw firsthand the salvation of the Lord as he and his people abode under the shadow of the Almighty while they marched out of Egypt, writing in Ps 91:8, "Only with thine eyes shalt though behold and see the reward of the wicked." Moses and the children of Israel did exactly what Ps 91:8 says: as they crossed the Red Sea, they looked back and saw the salvation of the Lord, watching as he overthrew both horse and rider in the sea. The benefits that God's people felt while under his shadow did not stop after their

---

2. Longman III, *Psalms*, 609.
3. Sarna, *On the Book of Psalms*, 105.

Red Sea crossing. Instead, for the next forty years, while roaming through the wilderness of sin, God would continue to provide for his people through many miracles—miracles such as water from a rock, manna each morning on the ground, and meat in the evening before they would turn in for the night. Thus, Ps 91 is Moses's testimony of his experience under the shadow of the Almighty as he makes his way from Egypt to Canaan.

Moses and the children of Israel, while under God's shadow, experienced a place of rest, a place of sustaining grace, a place of provision, a place of comfort, a place of direction, protection, and a place of deliverance as they made their way from the iron furnace of Egypt to the land of promise that God had provided for them. If there ever was a man who could paint a beautiful picture of God as a bulwark, shelter, and place of refuge whose shadow alone preserves his people, it is Moses. Therefore, Moses is the perfect person to be a tour guide for those who want to discover what life is like under the shadow of the Almighty. Psalm 91 is Moses's testimony, song, and praise unto the God of heaven, whose shadow alone sustains his people. So, let us allow Moses to take us on a tour under the shadow of the Almighty as we journey through Ps 91 together, hoping that we also can experience this wonderful life under the shadow of the Almighty. As Moses takes us on a tour under the shadow of the Almighty, the first place he shows us under God's shadow is a place of rest.

1

A Shadow of Rest
Psalm 91:1

INTRODUCTION

IF THERE EVER WAS a time in our world when folks needed a place of rest, not just any rest but continual rest from their fears, anxieties, and feelings of being overwhelmed, it is now. Now more than ever folks are longing for rest, a moment of peace, a slowdown in their lives where they can finally catch a breath. With anxiety levels at all-time highs due to the recent pandemic, financial hardships, ongoing wars, new wars, and a pivotal election on the horizon, folks have found themselves longing for relief more than they ever have. The last few years of one disaster in the world after another has wreaked havoc on the mental, physical, and spiritual health of people, including God's people. Christians who are promised a "peace that passeth all understanding" in Christ have found themselves in a state of panic, a state of worry, a state of never-ending wonder of what may happen next. Unfortunately, many Christians have forgotten that they have access to a rest that unbelievers do not, that is, an eternal rest that provides an eternal state of comfort in Christ through the promises that he has given in his word.

Rest has become a rare phenomenon, almost fictional, an impossibility that even Christians cannot seem to grasp. If there ever was a man who needed rest, if not more than we do now, it was Moses. Leading over a million Israelites through the many spiritual and physical valleys that would lay ahead of them as they traveled to the promised land, Moses may have felt that he would never find rest during this long journey. However, Moses, through witnessing miracle after miracle that God performed in liberating his people from Egyptian bondage, sees that it is the God of Israel that he can truly rest. While there are many places, such as clefts of rocks, that will provide Moses a place of protection in the desert from the enemy, Moses, however, describes a more excellent place of protection, a place where he found lodging and rest on his long journey to the promised land—under the shadow of the Almighty, according to v. 1.

In this psalm, Moses reminds those who follow Yahweh where their rest has always been, specifically, under the shadow of God. Moses will show in this psalm that this place of rest that surpasses all other areas of rest is exclusive to God's shadow and that there is no other that can provide such rest than the Almighty. This rest is exclusive in its location (under God's shadow); it is exclusive in its source (Yahweh), and this rest is also exclusive in how it is obtained. At the beginning of v. 1, Moses shows us that only those continually abiding in the "secret place of the Most High" will experience such rest under the shadow of the Almighty.

Verse 1 umbrellas the rest of Ps 91 as it introduces God's shadow as the place where one must abide to experience the remaining benefits presented in v. 2 through the remainder of Ps 91. It is under God's shadow that one will find rest, deliverance, protection, a life absent of fear, preservation, and so on. In the very first verse of Ps 91, Moses stirs our hearts by way of a reminder that those who continually abide with God will find themselves in a place of rest under the shadow of the Almighty. The first thing Moses does in v. 1 is show us the exclusivity of those who will find themselves resting under the shadow of the Almighty. Moses shows us that not everyone, not even every Christian, will find themselves resting in the shadow of the Almighty by indicating that only those who continually abide with the Most High will find this rest.

WHO WILL FIND REST? (V. 1A)

Moses opens this psalm with an indicative statement, not a command but a statement of fact, a promise, specifically that this rest will only be obtained by those who do this certain thing, namely abiding in the "secret places of the Most High." Verse 1 opens with a Qal participle verb, which will modify the main verb later in v. 1, the verb that speaks of "lodging or resting" in the shadow of the Almighty. As a Qal verb is non-modal, typically expressing an indicative mood that describes a real or factual action, Moses states that only those who carry out this action of abiding will find themselves in a place of rest under the shadow of the Almighty. The beginning of v. 1 shows us who it will be who will not only find rest under the shadow of the Almighty but also all the other benefits that Moses lists throughout the remainder of the psalm.

In v. 1, Moses says it is "he who is *abiding* [my translation of the participle *yoshab*] in the secret place of the Most High" who will experience life under God's shadow. In the original language, the sentence begins with the Qal verb *yoshab*, particularly a verbal adjective called a participle. As a participle, the verb *yoshab*, presented at the beginning of v. 1, modifies the main verb *yitlōwnān* found later in the verse. *Yoshab* modifies the main verb by explaining who will find themselves lodging or resting in the shadow of the Almighty. Therefore, this participle, *yoshab*, is explanatory or descriptive, emphasizing that a person's ongoing relationship with Yahweh will cause them to experience rest under his shadow. Thus, a translation closer to the original language may read, "He who is abiding or he who continually abides in the secret places of the Most High" will experience rest under the shadow of the Almighty. So, how can one find themselves under the shadow of the Almighty, and who will it be that will find this rest that Yahweh offers when they get there? Moses says it will only be those who are constantly abiding or dwelling with Yahweh.

The Greek Septuagint (LXX) translates *yoshab* as a present active participle, capturing the continual action of abiding that Moses describes. The LXX uses κατοικῶν as a translation of the Hebrew word *yoshab*. κατοικῶν stems from the root κατοικέω, meaning "settle in," "colonize," or "inhabit."[1] As a present active participle, κατοικῶν denotes a continual settling in, or a constant dwelling or inhabiting in the "secret place of the Most High," bringing that person into a place of rest under the shadow of the Almighty. In other words, those who are just acquainted with Yahweh, those who have simply tasted the goodness of Yahweh, or spent only a moment with Yahweh will not find themselves resting in Yahweh's shadow; only those who are abiding continually in the "secret places of the Most High" will experience rest in God's shadow.

Therefore, translating *yoshab* as "abiding" instead of simply "abide" properly denotes, as Moses intended, a continual action of spending time with God, communing with God, and walking with God. Based on the continuous state of this action, unfortunately, not all Christians will find this rest in God's shadow because they fail to abide with Yahweh continually. Some may converse with him sparingly, or maybe occasionally at the beginning of their conversion; either way, a volatile abiding with God simply will not suffice if one wants to find rest under his shadow. One must continually abide with Yahweh to experience the benefits of a life under his shadow. While living on earth, many know of Yahweh; Yahweh has saved many, but only a few will continually abide with him, thus experiencing this life of rest found under his shadow. For you to experience this rest, every minute of every day must be spent walking with God and abiding with him.

Interestingly, the Hebrew word for "abide" at the beginning of v. 1 does not denote past-tense action, nor a one-time event as some would like, because spending time with God occasionally is

---

1. Liddell et al., *Greek-English Lexicon*, 928.

much easier than spending time with him continually. Some would hope that the Christian life would be as easy as coming to saving faith and having all of the promises given in this psalm without the need to communicate with God continually. However, Moses says otherwise, that only those in constant communion with God will experience his constant rest under his shadow. Those who sparingly abide in Yahweh's word, who sparingly commune with him through prayer, and who sparingly mediate on his person must not expect to find this rest under the shadow of the Almighty.

Other translations may help understand the intimacy Moses is speaking of at the beginning of this verse. *Yoshab* can be translated as "abiding," "settling," "remaining," "inhabiting," or "sitting." The English version of the LXX translates v. 1 this way, detecting the participle at the beginning, saying, "The one *dwelling* in the support of the Most High, in the protection of the God of the heavens, that one will find lodging."[2] Moses quickly challenges his readers to take inventory of their communion with God in v. 1. Some questions arise in my mind when reading this first verse: Are you abiding with him, or has your time with God been spent sparingly? Do you ever wonder why you cannot find peace, rest, or assurance in your life even though you are a Christian? Pondering these questions forces us to take inventory of our lives, to see if we are abiding with God, to know if we are missing out on this unique rest that Moses mentions at the end of this verse. If v. 1 shows us anything as Christians, it shows us that there is no such thing as part-time Christianity; one must continually abide with God if one is going to truly experience God's blessings for those who are his. Moses encourages us early in this verse to constantly abide in the secret place of the Most High if we want to see God provide this unique rest in our lives, as he did in Moses. After showing us who will find themselves in the shadow of the Almighty, Moses now shows us where one must be abiding to bring oneself under the shadow of the Almighty.

---

2. Penner, *Lexham English Septuagint*, Ps 91:1. Emphasis added.

WHERE SHALL WE ABIDE? (V. 1B)

Those who are seeking true lasting rest will not find it in any created thing nor in any created being. Folks will not find this rest that God provides under his shadow in the places where most men lay their treasures, a place where Christ says "moth and rust doth corrupt, and where thieves break through and steal" (Matt 6:19). This rest cannot be found in the presence or shadow of kings, princes, or presidents, nor the bottom of a bottle, but only, exclusively in the "secret place of the Most High" one must dwell to find this rest under God's shadow. After explaining that only they who are abiding can find rest in the shadow of the Almighty, Moses doesn't leave us wondering where we are to be abiding but shows us that there is no other option but this one place—the "secret places of the Most High."

The word glossed with the English phrase "secret place" in the King James Version (KJV) is the Hebrew word *beseter*, which stems from the root *seter*, meaning a covering, hiding place, or a place of secrecy.[3] The attached *bet* denoting a definite article at the beginning of the word *seter* shows that the secret place Moses is referring to is not simply a secret place but *the* secret place. In other words, there is a specific secret place where, if one dwells there, one will find oneself under the shadow of the Almighty. This secret place that Moses refers to is exclusive to God only, meaning that it is in his secret place where one can find rest if they continually dwell there. The word is seen in Isa 28:17, which denotes a shelter that waters will overwhelm. Therefore, the word can be translated as "shelter," indicating that those who are "abiding in the shelter of the Most High" will be those who will find rest under his shadow. Psalm 81:7 uses the same word to denote a "secret place" where the thunder hides, saying, "Though calledst in trouble, and I delivered thee; I answered thee in the secret place of thunder." Regarding the Most High's secret place, Moses refers to the holy of holies, where God abides in a thick cloud of darkness in a confined place away from everyone except the high priest.

---

3. Brown et al., *Enhanced Brown-Driver-Briggs*, 712.

The tabernacle of the Lord, which housed the holy of holies, was first erected under Moses's leadership back in Exod 33:7, where the writer says, "And Moses took the tabernacle, and pitched it without the camp, afar off from camp, and called it the Tabernacle of the congregation. And it came to pass, that every one which sought the LORD went unto the tabernacle of the congregation, which was without the camp." Moses would be the first to enter the Lord's presence or dwell in his secret place before establishing Aaron and the remaining high priests as those who would have exclusive access to the holy of holies, thus being in the presence of God. Therefore, Moses was very familiar with this secret place where the presence of the God of Israel could be found. This secret place would eventually be where only the high priest could go within the tabernacle; it was the only place where God would dwell in a thick cloud of darkness amongst his people. The presence of God that was once seen and felt on and around Mount Sinai as God made himself known in a thick cloud of thunder and lightning now rested in a small room within a tabernacle with limited access from outsiders. God no longer dwelt outside this secret place within this tabernacle but only in this secret place called the holy of holies. To be in the presence of the Almighty, one had to be set apart as a high priest, and one could enter only once a year into the presence of the Most High.

Thankfully, in the case of believers today, all who are in Christ, our High Priest, have access to the holy of holies, the secret place of the Most High. As believers, we do not have to place our hope in a certain person to enter the holy of holies once a year on our behalf or come to God in general on our behalf, but, as Christians, we have complete access at any time to the Most High due to being in Christ, who is our High Priest. After Christ's death, burial, and resurrection, the veil separating believers from the holy of holies—the throne room where God dwells in heaven—was rent from top to bottom, providing believers access to the Most High. The dividing wall of hostility between God and man was wholly abolished in Christ, allowing us continual fellowship with God and the chance to abide in his presence if we choose to do so. Paul speaks of this access that both Jew and gentile believers have now into the presence of the Most High due to Christ's work on the cross. Paul says in Eph 2:14–16, "For he is our peace, who hath made both one, and hath broken down the middle wall of partition between us; Having abolished in his flesh the enmity, even the law of commandments contained in ordinances; for to make in himself of twain one new man, so making peace; And that he might reconcile both unto God in one body by the cross, having slain the enmity thereby." Therefore, through Christ, we have direct access at any time to the holy of holies where the Most High abides; thus, we have no excuse not to dwell or abide in the Most High's secret place, as Moses describes at the beginning of Ps 91.

All who are in Christ can come boldly at any time and abide continually in the presence of the Most High (Heb 4:14–16). We not only have access to this secret place, but we can come there boldly, knowing that God will welcome us there, welcoming us under his shadow where we can find rest for our souls. As sons and daughters of God, we can come at any time and abide in the presence of our Father because Jesus has made a way for us through his blood, which has washed us and made us clean so that we can stand before God and dwell in his presence. Under his shadow, we will find a shady place of rest and comfort. What Christ has done for his elect on the cross is wonderful, giving us direct access to the Father through him. Thus, we need no longer to rely upon a high priest to speak to God on our behalf nor travel to a building, a temple, or some physical location to be in the presence of the Lord; whoever is found in Christ can abide with him there. God's throne room is always open to his children, who can abide with him whenever and for however long they please. So, the ticket to entering that special rest under the shadow of the Almighty is communion with God through Christ; it is only through Christ that we have access to the secret place of the Most High.

The picture Moses paints of being in God's presence is beautiful. Imagine sitting with God, dwelling with him in his secret place, basking in the presence of the One who created the universe. It is easy to imagine dwelling with God when we understand that God wants to dwell with us. From the early chapters of Genesis, the Bible depicts God as a personal God who loves to dwell with his creation. The first chapters of Genesis describe God not as a faraway, distant God who creates and then leaves his creation to their own devices but as a God who creates in a way that allows him to abide with his creatures. The communing or abiding with God that Moses speaks of goes even further back before meeting with him in a small room in a tabernacle: God first abode with man and man with God immediately after creation. God personally created and gave life to the first man, Adam, but he did so in a special way by creating him in his image and breathing life into his nostrils.

One benefit of God creating man in his own image is that mankind can communicate with God. Like God, Adam could reason and speak and communicate; thus, he communicated with God frequently, unlike God's other creations, which were not made in his image. Therefore, early in the chapters of Genesis, we see the fulfillment of God's desire to create man so he could dwell with them. Daily, God walked with Adam, and Adam with God, giving us an early glimpse of what it was like to abide continually with God. Like God welcomed Adam to walk with him, God welcomes those who desire to abide with him today; in fact, he desires us to abide with him so much that he broke down that dividing wall of hostility between God and man through the death and resurrection of his Son Jesus Christ so we could have access to his presence once again. To allow us access back into his presence, the righteousness of his Son is imputed to us, while our sin is imputed to Christ and then abolished on the cross, leaving us spotless and without blemish before a holy God. Therefore, due to God's desire for us to abide with him once again as we once did in the garden, he would send his Son to wash away our sins and clean us up so we can once again stand in his presence.

The picture Moses paints early on of one dwelling in the secret place of the Most High is of one sitting with the God of heaven and experiencing the fresh rest that he offers under his shadow. Could you imagine sitting with the One who created the stars, who set the sun and the moon in their places? Could you imagine sitting with the One who Isaiah speaks of in Isa 40:12 as the One "who hath measured the waters in the hollow of his hand, and meted out heaven with the span, and comprehended the dust of the earth in a measure, and weighed the mountains in scales, and the hills in a balance?" Thankfully, Moses shows us early in this psalm that you can dwell with this powerful God and rest in his presence. In the next part of Ps 91:1, Moses shows that this rest under the shadow of the Almighty is promised or guaranteed to those who continually abide with him.

A PROMISED PLACE OF REST

The latter portion of this verse gives assurance and guarantees that those abiding in the Almighty's presence will find rest. Moses does not say in the latter part of this verse that those who are continually abiding in the secret place of the Most High *might* rest in the shadow of the Almighty, but he says that they *will* rest in this wonderful shadow. In the latter part of this verse, the main verb of the sentence, *lyn*, is introduced, modified by the participle "abiding" at the beginning of this verse. The Hebrew verb, *lyn*, is also a Qal verb, meaning it is active in voice and provides an unnuanced action—that of a current/continual resting or lodging. The verb is also written in the imperfect conjugation, expressing an incomplete action, and is usually translated with the English present tense. In other words, the verb for "rest" denotes a continual rest that will never be finished an active rest that has not simply occurred in the past but occurs continually to those who are abiding in the presence of the Most High. The root of this verb means to lodge, pass the night, or abide.[4] It's used in many places throughout Scripture—some seventy-one times—and is first seen in Gen 19:2 when Lot tells the angels that God sent to rescue his family, "My lords, please turn aside to your servant's house and *spend the night* and wash your feet" (ESV; emphasis added). Matthew Henry says regarding ps 91:1 "He who by faith chooses God

---

4. Brown et al., *Enhanced Brown-Driver-Briggs*, 533.

for his protector, will find all in him that he needs or can desire."⁵ Henry's words ring true with Moses's confirmation that those who abide continually in the presence of Yahweh will find what they need under his shadow—rest and a place of lodging from the weariness of this world.

As a statement of fact confirmed by using Qal verb stems throughout this verse, Moses assures the reader that they will find this place of rest or lodging if they continually abide with God. Therefore, the one who abides in God will never have to wonder or worry if God will hold up his end of the deal because Moses has written this statement indicatively, as a statement of fact. Therefore, it is guaranteed that if you are abiding with God, you will find rest in his shadow. For those who may wonder if there is any benefit in constantly communing with God, if there is any benefit in praying, fellowshiping, or abiding with God, Moses shows without question that those who do so will find a special rest as they have never experienced due to being under the shadow of the Almighty. Under his shadow, according to Moses, is a place of solitude, a place of lodging, a place of continual peace. The Hebrew word *lyn* paints a picture of one lodging peacefully during the night, awaiting the morning as a great storm passes.

Verse 1 comforts those facing some of their darkest hours because it promises that rest can be found and that rest is promised to those who will continually abide in him. For those on this long, tiresome journey called the Christian walk, who have faced one storm after another, Moses promises us that there is a place of lodging to provide shelter from the elements, and that place is under the shadow of the Almighty. Moses does not leave the reader clueless about whose shadow provides such a rest. Many wonder where true rest and peace that pass all understanding come from. Many may wonder who can provide such a rest in a time where rest is rarely found. In the last part of this verse, Moses reveals who provides a stable place to lay our heads when things around us are shaken, volatile, and wavering. The Almighty provides stability,

---

5. Henry, *Matthew Henry's Commentary*, 676.

whose shadow alone is enough to provide true rest for those who abide under it.

THE ONE WHOSE SHADOW PROVIDES REST (V. 1C)

The one who finds peace and rest during the darkest times of their life doesn't find it under the shadow of mighty men, the shadow of kings, the shadow of their spouse, the shadow of their physician, the shadow of their pride, nor the shadow of their own strength, but only under the shadow of the Almighty. Moses shows us that only the Almighty can be described as a shelter, as one who casts comforting shade, holds back or covers you from the turmoil that surrounds you, blankets you with peace, and blankets you with the assurance of his sovereignty. Moses shows the sheer power of the Almighty by showing us that his shadow alone provides peace and comfort for those who dwell in it. The New Testament reveals the power of Christ in a similar way. Christ's power was so great not only fully man but fully god that the hem of his garment alone, if touched by someone with true faith, was enough to heal them of their disease. In Mark's Gospel, a lady with an issue of blood for twelve years comes to Jesus by faith, understanding his power is so great that if she could just touch the hem of his garment, she would be healed. She makes her way through the crowds, her faith carrying her every step of the way, and immediately, when she touches Christ's garment, Jesus feels that power has gone out from him. Mark 5:30 gives the account of Jesus's power leaving him after this woman touches his garment, saying, "And Jesus, immediately knowing in himself that virtue had gone out of him, turned him about in the press, and said, Who touched my clothes?" The narrative continues, and Jesus finally realizes that it was a young woman who had an issue of blood for twelve years whose faith carried her to him just to touch his garment. As she fell at his feet, healed from her infirmity, Jesus noticed her great faith and said, "Daughter, thy faith hath made thee whole; go in peace, and be whole of thy plague" (Mark 5:34). Just as the garment of Christ was enough to provide healing to this woman due to her great faith, so God's shadow alone for those who abide in him is enough to provide a place of continual rest.

In other places in the Psalms, God's shadow is also shown to be a place of comfort and rest. In Ps 57:1, the psalmist describes God's powerful protection over his people, painting him as a bird who protects his young by covering them in the shadow of his wings, saying, "Be merciful unto me, O God, be merciful unto me: for my soul trusteth in thee: yea, in the shadow of thy wings will I make my refuge, until these calamities be overpast." Another popular place in Scripture where God's covering or blanketing of his people provides rest and protection from the enemy is seen in Exod 12. In Exod 12, God passes over or covers the houses of those who had blood on the doorpost. Guarding them by covering them, God gives them rest from the death angel that swept through Egypt, taking the firstborn of all who did not have the blood of a lamb over their doorposts. Exod 12:13 provides the account of God's covering or overshadowing of his people to protect them and give rest from the enemy, saying, "And the blood shall be to you for a token upon the houses where ye are: and when I see the blood, I will pass over you, and the plague shall not be upon you to destroy you, when I smite the land of Egypt." It is his shadow that provides peace; it blankets those who abide in him, not allowing any harm to come upon them, and provides them rest from their journey through this land.

CONCLUSION

It was the shadow of the cloud by day that Yahweh provided to cover the children of Israel, providing them cool shade and protection from the scorching heat as they made their way through the wilderness to the promised land. Today, it is the blood of Christ that covers those who are God's and provides them comfort and peace amid even the darkest of times because his blood guarantees that kingdom of heaven is theirs currently (Matt 5:3). The salvation that Christ gives through his cross provides us with rest and peace as we make our way through this world because it gives us a living hope, a hope in our promised inheritance that is being kept in heaven for us, a hope that we will make it to heaven by the preserving power of God (1 Pet 1:3–6). It is his blood that covers us, like God covered the Israelites, sheltering us from his wrath through Christ, who endures our wrath in our place (Isa 53:10). Christ's blood blankets us with the assurance of eternal life. His blood provides us with peace that surpasses all understanding and rest amid this Christian walk because we know we have peace with God and are his children because of what Christ did on the cross for us. We can rest in his shed blood because through his conquering over death and sin, we, too, through him, also conquer (Rom 8:37). Under his shadow, we must reside if we are going to walk through the valley of the shadow of death in peace. As we abide with him through the many valleys we may tread, we find comfort because it is his rod and staff that comfort us (Ps 23:4).

The word for "Almighty" is *El Shaddai* in Hebrew, showing us that this is the same God who walked with Abraham and comforted him. The Almighty is the same God who comforted Jacob amid many times of despair. Scripture shows us that no one else can bear the name "Almighty"; therefore, no one else's shadow can provide such a secure place of lodging and rest. Thus, when suffering comes, we must abide exclusively in him; if we want to suffer well and endure the suffering, we have been appointed. When doubt sets in and when fear vexes you, abide in him. If you abide in him, you will find rest because you will find yourself under his comforting shadow. Maybe it is easier to digest the magnitude of this verse if rendered this way: "Blessed is the man who continually dwells in the secret place of the Almighty; he will lodge peacefully in the shadow of the Almighty." Blessed or flourishing you will be if you continually abide in the presence of the Most High. As a Christian, there is no sweeter place to be; there is no safer place to live and abide than under the shadow of the Almighty.

2

A Shadow of Deliverance
Psalm 91:2–3

INTRODUCTION

IN 1529, GERMAN THEOLOGIAN and Reformer Martin Luther, who sparked the Protestant Reformation, penned the hymn "A Mighty Fortress Is Our God" as a paraphrase of Ps 46. This hymn emphasizes God's strength, protection, and deliverance, which he provides to his people during their most significant trials and afflictions. During a period of intense political and religious strife in Europe, which included the expansion of the Ottoman Empire into Eastern Europe, Luther would pen this famous hymn that screams God's deliverance to his believers. Drawing from the Psalms depicting God as a refuge, a bulwark, and a fortress, such as Ps 46, Luther found solace and comfort in these images of God that these psalmists painted. His reflection upon psalms such as Ps 46 would aid Luther in navigating the rough waters of life in such turbulent times. "A Mighty Fortress Is Our God" would become an anthem for Protestant Christians, a banner offering comfort and hope to believers wading through life's dark valleys. Today, the words of this hymn remain a source of encouragement, reminding us that our strength, resilience, and deliverance come not from ourselves, kings, or princes but from God, whose shadow alone provides a place of rest and refuge.

The first verse in Luther's hymn reaffirms the words of Ps 46 and others, including Ps 91, which describe God as a bulwark, a fortress, and a God who delivers his people. The first verse rings loudly, echoing many of the psalms describing God as an invincible battering ram that protects and delivers his people. Verse 1 of Luther's hymn triumphantly declares, "A Mighty fortress is our God, A bulwark never failing; Our helper he, amid the flood, of mortal ills prevailing."[1] As this hymn stems or has its roots in Ps 46 and Ps 91, it affirms that it is Yahweh alone, who is our place of shelter and deliverance, a place that cannot be shaken, where we can abide in safety. Like Ps 46 in which Luther derived his wonderful hymn, Ps 91 describes this place of shelter and stability as being under the shadow of the Almighty. If there were anyone who would agree with the words of Luther, it would be Moses, who penned similar words describing the God of heaven in Ps 91. It is under this shadow that Moses experienced God as Luther describes him: as a "bulwark never failing."

One of the clearest demonstrations of God as a fortress that Moses and the sons of Israel would experience is found in Exod 14. As the Israelites stood on the brink of destruction, ahead of them a wall of water, which was the Red Sea, and behind them a wall of hostile Egyptians. Having no way of escape, it would be Yahweh alone who would come to their rescue. The Egyptian army was salivating for the death of all those who belonged to Yahweh because Yahweh had just slaughtered all their firstborn sons and took away their Israelite slaves. The sons of Israel were surrounded from all sides between the Red Sea and an angry Egyptian army. There seemed to be no pathway to delivery. In such a dire moment, God showed himself as the deliverer of Israel, fortifying his title as a bulwark and a fortress to his people. It is Exod 14 where Moses testifies of God's successful parting of the Red Sea, enabling his

---

1. Luther, "Mighty Fortress Is Our God," 216.

people to safely walk across while he closes the same Red Sea on the Egyptians attempting to pursue them. Thus, Moses provides one of the most remarkable accounts of God's delivering power in history.

After Israel departs from Egypt through God's delivering power, Pharaoh is hot on their trail, seeking vengeance upon those who belong to Yahweh. We read of Pharaoh's pursuit of Israel through Moses's testimony in Exod 14:10, where he says, "And when Pharaoh drew nigh, the children of Israel lifted up their eyes, and, behold, the Egyptians marched after them; and they were sore afraid: and the children of Israel cried out unto the Lord." With Pharaoh and his army approaching quickly and with a wall of sea in front of them, the Israelites began to question God's delivering power, saying to Moses, "Because there were no graves in Egypt, hast thou taken us away to die in the wilderness? wherefore hast thou dealt thus with us, to carry us forth out of Egypt?" (Exod 14:11). Moses, trusting in God to once again demonstrate his delivering power, says, "fear ye not, stand still, and see the salvation of the Lord, which he will shew to you to day: for the Egyptians whom ye have seen to day, ye shall see them again no more for ever" (Exod 14:13). Moses then makes a statement validating Luther's claim that God is "a bulwark never failing," saying to the Israelites, "The Lord shall fight for you, and ye shall hold your peace" (Exod 14:14). In other words, don't worry, don't be afraid, and don't panic, because God will fight for you. Interestingly, Moses's claim that Yahweh will fight for you is further expounded upon in Ps 91. In v. 3, Moses declares that Yahweh "will deliver thee from the snare of the fowler," emphasizing God's protective power. Then, in v. 7, Moses expands on this, saying that due to Yahweh's delivering power, "A thousand shall fall at thy side, and ten thousand at thy right hand." This underscores the overwhelming strength of God's protection and deliverance. Throughout Moses's life, he watched as Yahweh gave him victory over many of his enemies.

After Moses claims victory through Yahweh, Yahweh fights on Israel's behalf. Watching the Egyptians draw closer to the frightened Israelites, Moses is about to witness firsthand God's delivering power. Moses's account of God's delivering power and God's work in preserving Israel in this moment prompts Moses to write Ps 91 as a testimony of what he saw the Lord do for his people. As the enemy drew closer, Moses obeyed the Lord by raising his staff and stretching out his hand over the Red Sea. In response, Yahweh began to bring about one of Israel's greatest deliverances, which they had experienced since their inception. Yahweh sent a strong wind that swept across the Red Sea, parting the waters and leaving them towering on each side of a dry path. Now, looking ahead of them to the dry ground that was once a sea, they saw the miraculous salvation of the Lord continuing to unfold before their eyes. What was once an impassable wall of water now was a dry path to salvation stretched out before them. Standing there in awe and wonder, Moses had just witnessed an undeniable demonstration of Yahweh's delivering power.

As they began to make their way across the dry earth, looking at a wall of water on each side, the Egyptians also entered on dry ground as they continued their pursuit. Thankfully, for the sake of Israel, Yahweh is not finished showing himself as their fortress and deliverer. Exodus 14:24–25 provides the account of Yahweh's intervention on behalf of Israel, saying, "And it came to pass, that in the morning watch the Lord looked unto the host of the Egyptians through the pillar of fire and of the cloud, and troubled the host of the Egyptians, And took off their chariot wheels, that they drave them heavily: so that the Egyptians said, Let us flee from the face of Israel; for the Lord fighteth for them against the Egyptians." Yahweh would not let them escape easily, but as Moses writes in Ps 91, the enemy would be paid their due recompense, and these Egyptians would obtain what was due to them from Yahweh at the bottom of the Red Sea.

In a last-ditch effort to escape the wrath of Yahweh, the Egyptians saw their pathway to victory dissolving quickly, so they turned back to Egypt amid the dry ground of the sea, hoping to make it back to shore. Yahweh, in his fury, released the walls of the sea that stood on both sides of the Egyptians, allowing the water to enclose upon them, swallowing up all those who attempted to kill

God's people. Pharaoh and the Egyptian army were destroyed in an instant by the hand of Yahweh. Exodus 14:28, 30–31 provides the dramatic account of Pharaoh's demise, saying, "And the waters returned, and covered the chariots, and the horsemen, and all the host of Pharaoh that came into the sea after them; there remained not so much as one of them. . . . Thus the LORD saved Israel that day out of the hand of the Egyptians; and Israel saw the Egyptians dead upon the sea shore. And Israel saw that great work which the LORD did upon the Egyptians: and the people feared the LORD, and believed the LORD, and his servant Moses." Firsthand, the sons of Israel and Moses experienced life under the shadow of God. In their experience, God delivered his people, acting as a siege wall surrounding his people, a battering ram destroying the enemy of his people and bringing swift deliverance.

If there was ever a man who could paint the God of heaven as the sole source of deliverance for his people from their enemies, the One whose shadow alone offers rest and salvation from all adversaries, it was Moses. Psalm 91 is Moses's powerful portrait of Yahweh as Israel's deliverer God. Just as Luther's hymn, "A Mighty Fortress Is Our God," became an anthem of hope for Protestant Christians, Ps 91 serves the same as an anthem penned by Moses, offering all who read it a profound assurance of God's delivering power. Even today, Ps 91 remains a treasured passage for those facing affliction. Its timeless truths resound with the promise that God's shadow alone provides a place of rest while also offering a place of deliverance. This hymn of Moses, namely Ps 91, is rooted in the Exodus account as Israel made their way to the promised land, abiding under the shadow of the Almighty. Let's look closely at vv. 2–3 of this wonderful hymn by Moses, which continues giving us this tour of life under the shadow of the Almighty. As Moses brings us to vv. 2–3, we see that under God's shadow, one will experience his delivering power.

THE IDENTITY OF OUR DELIVERER (V. 2)

Before Moses demonstrates how God works in our deliverance under his shadow, he first emphasizes who it is whose shadow provides such protection and deliverance. This foundational truth must be established first—before we consider God's mighty works, we must know the God under whose shadow we dwell. In v. 2, Moses begins by offering praise and adoration to only One, specifically, the God he calls "his refuge, his fortress, and his God." Moses shows us immediately that these titles are shared with no one else but the God of Israel, who delivered him from Egyptian bondage. Moses does not abide with just any god but the One true God, the eternal God of Israel, who has proven himself to Moses many times as the One who delivers his people.

By using two titles for God, namely the Most High and the Almighty in v. 1, then using his covenantal name in v. 2, Moses emphatically shows there is no other that can hold such titles as "refuge," "fortress," or "deliverer" except this One named Yahweh. No king, no prince, and indeed no false god can ever bear such titles as "refuge" or "fortress" as Yahweh can. By emphatically giving one title after another to Yahweh, Moses makes sure that there is no doubt that Yahweh's shadow alone provides such benefits. This name, Yahweh, that Moses gives in v. 2 is the name by which Moses first knew God. As Moses looked at the burning bush that spoke to him concerning Israel, he asked for the name of the One speaking to him. God's voice thunders from the flames that engulfed the bush, saying in Exod 3:14, "I Am That I Am: and he said, Thus shalt thou say unto the children of Israel, I Am hath sent me unto you." The name "I Am" speaks of God's self-existence, along with his covenantal name that he gives a few verses down in Exod 3:16, saying, "Go, and gather the elders of Israel together, and say unto them, The Lord [Yahweh] God of your fathers, the God of Abraham, of Isaac, and of Jacob, appeared unto me, saying, I have surely visited you, and seen that which is done to you in Egypt." His eternal nature, his self-existence, and all of his remaining attributes are wrapped up in this name. It is this Yahweh God who has no beginning and no end, who is the self-sustaining, self-existent God that Moses is speaking of here in Ps 91.

The burning bush experience was not the first time Moses was met with the power of God; however, as a young infant, Moses experienced the delivering power of God. It is this God, Yahweh, whose shadow protected Moses as an infant, who worked in the heart of his mother to place him in a basket of bulrushes and send him down the river to escape Pharaoh's decree to kill all the Israelite male children. As Moses drifted along in the river, still almost a newborn, in God's providence, Pharaoh's daughter found him and adopted him as her own, raising him in the house of Pharaoh. God's delivering power would be seen countless times in the life of Moses. Under the shelter of Yahweh's shadow, Moses would later witness the miraculous plagues upon Egypt, the parting of the Red Sea, the pillar of fire by night and the cloud by day that Yahweh gave to both guide and shade the sons of Israel as they traveled to the promised land. Moses would also see the miracle of water coming forth from a rock, manna appearing in the desert, and meat to eat at night that came directly from God, proving God's deliverance and provision for his people.

Perhaps the most powerful moment when Moses encounters God is his encounter with Yahweh on Mount Sinai after Israel's deliverance from Egypt. As Moses drew close to Mount Sinai to receive the Ten Commandments from God, the Lord's voice thundered from the mountain, revealing himself to Moses in flashes of lightning and thick clouds of smoke. In this awe-inspiring moment, Moses was reminded of the overwhelming power of God. It is this same power Moses saw firsthand that Moses describes in Ps 91 as the power God uses to deliver for his people who abide under his shadow. Having established Yahweh alone, whom Moses knew so well, as the source of deliverance, Moses declares confidently, "He is my refuge and my fortress: my God; in him will I trust" (Ps 91:2). Not once in v. 2 does Moses credit any such names to humans or any other created thing, but this Yahweh alone. However, Moses's expression of trust in Yahweh is not isolated; many others in

Scripture validate Moses's titles for God by acknowledging God's delivering power.

King David, like Moses, finds refuge in the God of Israel alone and repeatedly affirms this in the Psalms. David, like Moses, understood Yahweh as a shield, a refuge, and a fortress, declaring in Ps 3:3, "But thou, O LORD, art a shield for me." In this psalm, David speaks of God as the One who sustains him, lifts his head, and shatters the teeth of the wicked. David shows that his salvation belongs to Yahweh throughout this psalm. In Ps 5:12, David, speaking directly to God, says, "For thou, LORD, wilt bless the righteous; with favour wilt thou compass him as with a shield," Using the second person masculine singular for the verb *tebarek*, meaning "will bless," David shows that this blessing comes from Yahweh alone, who is the singular agent of this action. David does not say that Yahweh and his angels provide this blessing and protection, nor does David add any human to the mix, but Yahweh alone provides this great deliverance to his people.

David's confidence in God's deliverance is also expressed in Ps 7:1 when he says, "O LORD my God, in thee do I put my trust." Right out of the gate, David acknowledges that there is no refuge or source of protection other than God alone. David knows that only God has the power to deliver him, and he asks God to save him from those who pursue him in the remainder of this psalm. In Ps 18:1–2, David echoes Moses, giving a remarkable list of names and titles for Yahweh, saying, "I will love thee, O LORD, my strength. The LORD is my rock, and my fortress, and my deliverer; My God, my strength, in whom I will trust; my buckler, and the horn of my salvation, and my high tower." These names reflect the multifaceted nature of God's deliverance, showing that any great delivering noun we can think of could be an excellent title for God. So, not only to Moses but to David and many others, Yahweh is his people's ultimate refuge, shelter, and strength. In many other places throughout the Psalms, David sings aloud about the delivering power of Yahweh, as does Moses in Ps 91. In Ps 28:7, David declares, "The LORD is my strength and my shield." In Ps 33:20, he affirms, "Our soul waiteth for the LORD: he is our help and our shield." In other psalms, such as in Ps 57:1, where David prays, "Be merciful to me, O God, be merciful unto me: For my soul trusteth in thee," David continues to show, as he does throughout the Psalter, his trust in the delivering power of Yahweh. These repeated affirmations throughout the Psalms make it clear that Moses is right that safety, strength, and deliverance are exclusively found under the shadow of the Almighty.

The shadow of God is not a mere metaphor but a place of absolute, tangible protection that both Moses and David speak of many times. Moses and David understood that only those who trust Yahweh will experience him as a bulwark and fortress. If there is one thing both Moses and David make clear in their psalms, especially Moses's Ps 91, it is that there is no earthly power, no human authority, and no false god that can provide the kind of protection that Yahweh offers. Yahweh's shadow is a place where we can safely lodge, where our enemies cannot touch us, and where he delivers us from the storms of life.

It is by the great rest that God's shadow provides and the great deliverance found under his shadow that Moses can say later in v. 5 that those who abide under this shadow can live a life absent of fear. Moses affirms one of the greatest promises concerning those living under Yahweh's shadow, saying in v. 5, "Thou shalt not be afraid." Here, Moses assures those who dwell under the shadow of the Almighty that they do not need to fear because God is their refuge, their fortress, and God will deliver them. Moses, David, and the psalmists all point us to the same truth: only Yahweh delivers. Under his shadow, we find true refuge and deliverance from the Evil One and our enemies. As we reflect on these truths, let us take comfort in knowing that we, too, are invited to rest in the shadow of the Almighty, where fear cannot reach us, and deliverance is assured. So how does God deliver those who abide under his shadow? Moses answers this question in the latter part of v. 2 and v. 3.

THE WORKS OF OUR DELIVERER (V. 3)

Moses now transitions in v. 2 from the first person, saying "my God is" in v. 2, to the third person in v. 3, telling us that it is "he" (this God) alone who delivers, protects, and gives recompense to our enemies. Using the third person singular when describing God's actions, Moses emphasizes God's exclusive, personal, and sovereign role in delivering his people. The Hebrew text employs the third person singular to emphasize the exclusive, personal, and sovereign role of God in delivering his people.

Moses confidently says, "Surely he shall deliver thee," giving his readers little doubt that one can find a sure deliverance under the shadow of the Almighty. At the beginning of v. 3, the Hebrew particle *ki*, often translated as "for" or "surely," as in the KJV, is a conjunction connecting the previous section with v. 3. The word translated "surely" or "for" is an explanatory conjunction, essentially saying "for it is this God"—whose shadow provides rest in v. 1 and who Moses calls his refuge and fortress in v. 2—this is the One who delivers. The particle *ki* can also act as a declaration of certainty as it is used in the KJV in this verse, showing that Moses is sure that his God will deliver those who abide under his shadow. Either way, Moses leaves no doubt that God not only provides rest for those who dwell under his shadow but also will provide deliverance.

Notice immediately that Moses makes it clear that true deliverance is exclusive to this God alone, the one true God. He uses the third person singular—not plural—to show us that no one can accomplish such deliverance. Moses doesn't say, "For it is he and his angels who deliver you," or, "For it is he and your wit that delivers you," or, "For it is he and mighty men, kings, and princes who deliver you." No; our deliverance is exclusive to the God of heaven. In the Old Testament, God has shown himself to be the only deliverer of his people. As God is a jealous God, he will not share his title as deliverer with anyone else. In the book of Exodus, he repeatedly tells Moses that he is going to harden Pharaoh's heart to make it impossible for anyone else to deliver the Israelites from Pharaoh but God alone, all to make his name great.

Over and over, God says to Moses that Egypt will know that he is Yahweh, that Israel will know that he is the Lord, or that what he is going to do, he is doing for his name's sake. God wants to be known as the only way, path, and hope for those whom he will deliver. In Exod 7:5, Yahweh says, "And the Egyptians shall know that I am the LORD, when I stretch forth mine hand upon Egypt, and bring out the children of Israel from among them." Suppose it is unclear that God wants his power and sovereignty to be known by all peoples. In that case, God says again he wants his name to be known in Exod 9:16. In Exod 9:16, God says to Pharaoh through Moses, "And in very deed for this cause have I raised thee up, for to shew in thee my power; and that my name may be declared throughout all the earth." In many places, God shows that he wants his name to be known and glorified, thus orchestrating events that will ultimately give glory to his name. In Ps 23, for example, David says that the Lord leads us in the paths of righteousness "for his name's sake." Knowing that deliverance can come through no other but the God of heaven, Moses gives full accreditation to God, as the only one who can deliver his people in v. 3.

In our greatest salvation—the salvation of our souls—this is also made clear: there is no other way to have our sins forgiven, no other who can save us from our sins except the Lord Jesus Christ. It is Jesus, whose blood alone (not the blood of bulls or goats), whose atonement alone, provides forgiveness and remission of sins. God the Son had to come in the form of sinful man to deliver us because we couldn't deliver ourselves. Therefore, even in the salvation of our souls, we must boast in God alone and never in ourselves. It is not God and man that deliver us from our sins. It is not God and our will that brings us to Christ to be forgiven of our sins. It is not God and the Pope nor God and some priest that work together to bring about our salvation. It is God alone who saves sinners and delivers sinners. Just as the Pharisees rightly said, "Who can forgive sins but God only?" (Mark 2:7). When they saw Jesus forgive the paralytic's sins, we too must recognize that God alone has the authority to forgive sins.

While Moses, in context, speaks more of physical enemies, we must not forget that God's greatest delivery is not from our physical enemies but our spiritual enemies, which are indwelling sins and the accuser of the brethren. Just as there was no other name under heaven that could save Moses and Israel from Egypt, there is no other name under heaven today that can save folks from their sin. Acts 4:12 says, "Neither is there salvation in any other: for there is none other name under heaven given among men, whereby we must be saved." Any deliverance we experience, especially the salvation of our souls, is exclusive to the God of Israel, Yahweh. There is no other that could pay our ransom, bear our cross, conquer death and the grave, and provide us with eternal life but this God, who came personally in the flesh to save his people.

Therefore, under the shadow of the Almighty, we find even the deliverance of our souls. Moses makes it clear that we find true deliverance only in the shadow of this God. In the remainder of v. 3, Moses continues to show us what God delivers us from. Moses covers a range of potential enemies that may try to harm us, saying that God delivers us not only from the "snare of the trapper" but also from the "pestilence." Using such a range of enemies, Moses shows us that from the greatest to the least of our enemies—whether external enemies, internal struggles like disease and pestilence, or even our spiritual enemies, namely Satan and sin—God can deliver us from them all if he wills to do so. Under the shadow of God, we find deliverance from every type of enemy that may afflict us. Moses speaks of a great enemy of God's people called "the trapper" or "the fowler," depending on what translation you read. This fowler is one who sets snares to capture us daily like a fowler sets traps to catch birds. Skilled in trapping, this evil fowler lures his prey into traps seeking to destroy and lead them into failure. This trapper represents our greatest enemy, Satan.

Satan is the great deceiver, the one who sets traps before us daily, attempting to destroy God's people. Yet Moses assures us that under the shadow of the Almighty, there is deliverance from the snares of this great enemy. Jesus affirms this deliverance in the Lord's Prayer, referring to Satan as the "Evil One" from whom God alone delivers us. Teaching his disciples how to pray, Jesus models the petition, urging us to pray daily for God to deliver us from the "Evil One." We cannot deliver ourselves from the Evil One, nor can we fight him off, resist him, or rebuke him in our own strength. The only One who has the power, the authority, and the ability to rebuke and deliver you from the schemes of the Devil and the traps that he sets before us is this God in whom Moses calls "the Most High," "the Almighty," his "refuge," his "fortress," his "God," namely, the God of heaven.

CONCLUSION

Matthew Henry writes, "The spiritual life is protected by divine grace from the temptations of Satan, which are as snares of the fowler, and from the contagion of sin, which is a noisome pestilence. Great security is promised to believers amid danger."[2] If you are seeking rest, longing for a place of refuge, a mighty fortress where you can be secure from your enemies—then abide in the shadow of the Almighty. Find yourself under his protective shadow, for only there will you find peace and a place where fear cannot touch you. His shadow blankets us with rest, acts as a fortress and a stronghold to deliver us from our enemies, and shields us from the endless arrows of the Wicked One. It is a place where fear cannot abide, and the enemy cannot gain ground. Therefore, let us seek deliverance under his shadow.

---

2. Henry, *Matthew Henry's Exposition*, 200.

3

A Life Lived Under God's Protection

Psalm 51:4

INTRODUCTION

As OUR TOUR GUIDE through a life under the shadow of the Almighty, Moses has already shown us that under the shadow of the Almighty is a life of rest and a life of deliverance. While on this tour, Moses earlier demonstrated that the key to living under the shadow of the Almighty is to abide with God continually, according to v. 1 of Ps 91. So, before he shows us all the special places under the shadow of the Almighty, Moses shows us how we are to enter such a place, namely by continually abiding in the secret places of the Most High. As an indicative statement or a statement of fact, Moses opens up this wonderful psalm, showing us that all the precious promises that life under the shadow of the Almighty provides are only for those who continually abide in the secret place of the Most High. It is as if Moses is saying, "Did you know that he who is abiding in the secret places of the Most High will receive these wonderful benefits that come with living under the shadow of the Almighty?"

As mentioned in the previous chapter, the word "abides" or "dwells" in Ps 91, depending on the translation, needs to be examined closely; Moses never says that "he who has abided in the shelter or secret places of the Most High will find rest in the shadow of the Almighty" or "he that will abide will find rest under the shadow of the Almighty," but rather, only those who are "continually abiding in the secret place of the Most High will find continual rest under the shadow of the Almighty." As Moses continues into vv. 2–3, he also shows that those who continually abide with the Most High will find deliverance under his shadow. Moses makes it clear using the covenant name of God, namely Yahweh, that this deliverance found under the shadow of the Almighty is exclusive to Yahweh. In other words, only Yahweh God, the one in whom Moses calls his refuge and fortress, provides such great deliverance from the "snare of the fowler, and from the noisome pestilence" (Ps 91:3). However, as Moses continues conducting his tour of life under the shadow of the Almighty, he demonstrates in v. 4 that this life is marked by Yahweh's protection.

Moses's life can be summarized as one that continually relied upon Yahweh, seeking and abiding with him. From the moment he encountered God in the burning bush; to his meetings with Yahweh on Mount Sinai surrounded by smoke, thunder, and lightning; to obeying God in delivering plague after plague upon Pharaoh; and through crossing the Red Sea and wandering in the desert, Moses experienced firsthand how sweet life is under the shadow of the Almighty. Moses understood the importance of constant communion with God. If there was an example of one who continually dwelled in the "secret places of the Most High," it was Moses. Abiding in God's presence provided him with direction, encouragement, wisdom, deliverance, and protection—just as the opening verses of this psalm describe the benefits of dwelling in Yahweh's shadow.

Moses knew that for the sustaining and success of the mission that God had ordered him to complete, he must remain in continual dependence on God. If he was to lead over a million people from the iron furnace of Egypt to the edge of the promised land, he could not do so apart from abiding in the presence of Yahweh. This unbroken relationship with the Almighty fueled Moses's leadership and perseverance; Moses's sustaining was due to his living under the shadow of the Almighty. Moses experienced firsthand the rest, deliverance, and protection he mentions under this great shadow of the Almighty. So, we must take it to heart when Moses essentially says, "You won't find these wonderful benefits that I have experienced under anyone else's shadow, nor will you obtain them from abiding with anyone else; but true rest, deliverance and protection is found exclusively with the Almighty and under his shadow." Moses could accredit no other for his and his people's deliverance from Egypt but the God of Israel. So, he makes it clear on this tour through Ps 91 that only his God, whom he trusts (v. 3), provides all of these precious benefits.

To show that this rest, deliverance, and protection is exclusive to the God that led Moses and his people out of Egypt, Moses uses many names attributed to Yahweh. Beginning in v. 1, he speaks of Yahweh as the Most High. The name "Most High" signifies his sovereignty and dominion over all creation, being high above all things; this name emphasizes his uniqueness, and no other being is given such a title. It is Yahweh's power, holiness, and all of his attributes present with him that are always carried out to the highest degree. As the Most High, no one can be as merciful, gracious, or protecting, nor offer such a great deliverance or an extraordinary life under his shadow, as this Most High God. Therefore, as Moses continues to show us what life is like under the shadow of the Almighty, the question arises, "Why would you want to abide with anyone else but the One whose benefits are given to the highest degree because they come from the Most High, namely Yahweh?" Kings, princes, and presidents cannot offer what this God provides to those who abide with him. So, Ps 91 is Moses's way of saying, "Here is what you will find when you abide in the secret places of this Most High God; you will find things like rest, deliverance, and protection to the utmost degree."

A Life Lived Under God's Protection

To understand this point more fully, it is necessary to review the places we have been in Moses's tour of life under the shadow of the Almighty. The first place Moses takes us under Yahweh's shadow is a place of rest. In v. 1, Moses shows us that rest, or a place of lodging, can be found under this wonderful shadow. The word for "rest" or "abide," as translated in the KJV, is written as an imperfect verb, meaning that this "rest" will never end because it is a continual rest. So those who are abiding in the secret place of the Most High will find a continual rest under the shadow of the Almighty. The "rest" described here is more than just a peaceful state; it signifies a place of refuge, a lodging where one can find shelter from a storm. Moses paints this place of rest as a sanctuary, a place to spend the night away from the elements, the turmoil, and the distractions of the world around us. The shadow of the Almighty is a haven for those who want to escape the noise and busyness of life. It is only here that true peace is found in the presence of the Almighty, a peace that provides rest for the weary heart.

If this life under Yahweh's shadow does not sound sweet so far, Moses continues his tour in v. 2 to illustrate that not only rest can be found under this great shadow but deliverance as well. The deliverance Moses speaks of in v. 2 is a complete deliverance of both soul and body from the "snare of the fowler and from noisome pestilence" mentioned in v. 3. It is the Evil One, namely Satan, that many commentators, such as Matthew Henry, Charles Spurgeon, and John Gill, believe is the "fowler" that Moses refers to in v. 3. Commentator Matthew Henry, in his commentary on Ps 91, states regarding the "fowler" that it is "Satan, who lays snares for the soul, in order to deceive and destroy it."[1] In his commentary, Henry parallels the "snare of the fowler" and the traps Satan sets for the faithful through temptation and deceit. In Spurgeon's wonderful commentary on the Psalms, *The Treasury of David*, Spurgeon links the fowler to Satan, saying, "The fowler is a type of the enemy of souls, who continually lies in wait to ensnare the unwary."[2] John Gill follows both Henry and Spurgeon when he

---

1. Henry, *Matthew Henry's Commentary*, 807.
2. Spurgeon, *Treasury of David* 2, 31.

states in his commentary that the fowler refers to "the devil, who, like a bird-catcher, lays snares for men, to deceive them and bring them into destruction."[3] So only those who dwell under Yahweh's shadow will find deliverance from the greatest enemy that has ever come against humankind, namely Satan or the "fowler," as Moses calls him here.

As life is shown to be sweeter and sweeter under the shadow of the Almighty, Moses offers those who abide under this shadow another wonderful promise, namely that under this shadow, one will find God's unmatched protection. Henry's commentary summarizes this verse and its effect on believers who hold to its promises. Henry writes that, regarding God's protection, Moses mentions in v. 2 that "God is the refuge of his people, and as a hen gathers her chickens under her wings, so he spreads his wings over them. There is safety under God's wings, for his wings are strong and tender. The care of the Almighty is a sure shelter, and we are called to rest in his protection with full confidence."[4] Henry's observation at the end of his quote that "we are called to rest in his protection with full confidence" is particularly insightful. Henry seems to grasp that the rest mentioned in Ps 91:1 cannot be fully appreciated without the other benefits Moses mentions in the rest of the psalm. In other words, the rest found under the shadow of the Almighty stems from his promise to deliver and protect those who abide under his shadow. It is easy to rest in Yahweh, knowing that he will not only deliver you from the Evil One but protect you like a mother hen protects her chicks, which is how Moses describes God's protection in v. 4.

Moses already alluded to God's protection earlier in v. 2, calling Yahweh his "refuge" and "fortress." The word for "fortress" Moses uses in v. 2 provides more validity to the protection Yahweh offers. While most translations use the word "fortress," the word denotes a place of being held fast, namely a place where God will hold his own fast, not letting them go. God surrounds his people as a fortress, providing unmatched protection so they will not be

---

3. Gill, *Exposition of the Old Testament*, 459.
4. Henry, *Matthew Henry's Commentary*, 838.

harmed. The word "fortress" and the action of his protection echo what others in Scripture speak of when they describe the protection that Yahweh gives them when they describe Yahweh's protection as a hedge that he has placed around them.

As Satan speaks to Yahweh regarding Job and Job's continual worship of Yahweh, Satan falsely claims that Job continually worships because nothing ever harms Job or his family due to the hedge that God has placed around him. Satan mentions Yahweh's hedge of protection in his dialogue with Yahweh in Job 1:10, saying, "Hast not thou made an hedge about him, and about his house, and about all that he hath on every side? thou hast blessed the work of his hands, and his substance is increased in the land." Satan complains to Yahweh that Job's prospering is due to this hedge of protection that Yahweh has placed around Job. The removal of God's hedge of protection or his being a fortress to his people is seen as a judgment in Isaiah's prophecy towards Israel in Isa 5:5 when Isaiah speaks for Yahweh, saying, "And now go to; I will tell you what I will do to my vineyard: I will take away the hedge thereof, and it shall be eaten up; and break down the wall thereof, and it shall be trodden down." Isaiah prophesies that God is going to remove his hedge of protection from his people because of their continual turning to other gods and practicing of detestable acts. So, while sin separates those who abide in it from God's protection, it is those who continually abide under Yahweh's shadow that his protection will sustain.

Much Scripture validates that God places a hedge of protection around those who continually abide with him. The term "hedge" is found in the relationship between the shepherd and his sheep. As the chief shepherd, Yahweh protects his sheep, keeping them from those who seek to devour them by placing a hedge of protection around them. In ancient times, shepherds would place hedges of thorns and thistles around their flocks to protect them from predators and to keep them from straying from the safety of the sheepfold.[5] This image illustrates God's preserving protection: he not only guards his people from the enemy but also keeps them

---

5. Freeman, *Manners and Customs*, 451.

from wandering back into enemy territory, and particularly from returning to a life of sin. Moses, like others throughout Scripture, also validates God's protection of those who abide with him in v. 4 of Ps 91. Instead of a shepherd placing his sheep within a hedge of protection, Moses paints a picture of Yahweh as a mother bird or hen who gathers her children under her wing, offering them a place of refuge and protection. This wonderful picture of protection that Moses shows us can be found under the shadow of the Almighty.

THE PROMISE OF HIS PROTECTION (V. 4A)

As the reader reaches v. 4 of Ps 91, Moses continues to speak about Yahweh in the third person. In v. 2, Moses speaks declaring, "He is my refuge and my fortress: my God; in him will I trust." Moses continues referring to Yahweh in the third person saying, "He will cover thee with feathers, and under his wings shalt thou trust: his truth shall be thy shield and buckler," referring to Yahweh's actions and promises. Using the third person, Moses clarifies what Yahweh will do for those who abide under his shadow. Using the third person singular, Moses shows that it is this God alone, Yahweh God, who not only delivers his people from the snare of the fowler and the noisome pestilence but is also the one who will "cover you with his feathers" (v. 4). This statement serves a twofold purpose; first, as an indicative statement, it acts as a statement of fact, revealing that only this God can cover you and protect you in this manner. Secondly, the Hebrew verb *yasek* denotes a sure action that Yahweh will take upon those who abide under his shadow, making this statement from Moses a promise. *Yasek* is a Hif'il, imperfect, third-person, masculine, singular verb stemming from the root *sak*, meaning "to overshadow, screen, or cover."[6] In this verse, Hif'il verbs such as *yasek* are usually causative, meaning that this type of verb indicates that the subject is causing the action to happen. In the case of *yasek*, Yahweh (the subject) is causing the action

---

6. Brown et al., *Enhanced Brown-Driver-Briggs*, 696.

of protecting and covering to happen to those who abide under his shadow. Using the Hif'il verb *yasek*, Moses emphasizes Yahweh's actions in providing safety and refuge for his people by personally covering those who abide under his shadow. Another indicator that Moses's statement in v. 4 regarding Yahweh's protection is a promise is that the verb *yasek* is also written as an imperfect. As an imperfect, the action of covering that Moses mentions here can be both a present and future action that is continuous. Imperfect verbs denote incomplete actions that are continual in nature; these actions can be current actions or actions that will happen in the future. Therefore, based on the type of verb Moses uses in v. 4, those who abide in the shadow of the Almighty can guarantee that Yahweh will continually cover them with his protection.

As Moses uses the third person singular to refer to Yahweh, he emphasizes that Yahweh will personally cover his people. Just as Yahweh personally communed with Adam and Eve; just as God personally breathed the breath of life in them; just as God personally came to Moses in a burning bush, directing Moses in his deliverance of Israel from Egypt, Yahweh here in Ps 91:4 is portrayed as the personal protector of his people, covering them as a mother bird covers her children with her wings. Just as Yahweh walked with the Shadrach, Meshach, and Abednego in the fiery furnace, protecting them so they did not even have the stench of smoke upon them, Yahweh personally blankets those who abide under his shadow. No other god can offer such protection, such as covering, as Moses mentions here, other than Yahweh God. Many times, the Old Testament writers draw a contrast between the power of Yahweh and the power of man-made gods that many worshiped during the time of these writings.

The exclusiveness of Yahweh's delivering and protecting power is emphasized even further when compared to the false gods worshiped throughout the Old Testament. Throughout this psalm, Moses uses many names and titles for Yahweh to show that only the God of Israel can provide such a beautiful life for those who dwell in his shadow. Moses knew the dangers of following false gods and wanted to clarify that no other god can provide what

Yahweh can for those who abide in him. In fact, all of Scripture shows that Yahweh God is the only God who can deliver, protect, and provide for those who trust in him. The man-made gods of the Old Testament were cold and dead, figurines made with the hands and minds of men. It is these man-made gods that offered nothing to those who worshiped them. All Scripture, including Ps 91, affirms that only Yahweh God, who was neither made nor formulated by human hands but has always been, is the only one who can carry out such great deliverances and miracles like those recorded throughout the Old Testament. Psalm 115:4–8 describes the false security other gods offer by showing their inferiority to Yahweh God. The psalmist contrasts Yahweh and the false gods that have been worshiped throughout history, saying, "Their idols are silver and gold, the work of men's hands. They have mouths, but they speak not: eyes have they, but they see not; They have ears, but they hear not: noses have they, but they smell not: They have hands, but they handle not: feet have they, but they walk not: neither speak they through their throat. They that make them are like unto them; so is every one that trusteth in them." Made by human hands, these idols cannot offer the rest, deliverance, and protection that Moses ascribes to Yahweh in Ps 91. All other gods are dead, lifeless, and are simply man-made creations, while Yahweh alone is eternal, having no beginning, and is unmatched in his power. Yahweh's shadow outperforms any false god in the actions of deliverance, protection, and many other benefits that Yahweh gives throughout the Scripture. Therefore, we can be sure that if we are abiding under the shadow of the Almighty, we will receive a continual covering and blanketing of unmatched protection from Yahweh. There is no safer place than under the protection of the God of the universe.

THE EXTENT OF HIS PROTECTION (V. 4B)

To show the extent of God's protection, Moses uses a literary device called zoomorphism, which shows God as a bird who covers his own with his wings. While God is not a bird, the text uses animal-like imagery to describe his protective care in a way that is relatable. Moses's account of Yahweh as a bird covering his children with his wings is not the first time God is given animal-like qualities to describe some of his attributes. In fact, this is not the first time Moses has emphasized God's attributes using zoomorphism. In Deut 32:11–12, he compares God to an eagle. Deuteronomy 32:11–12 is a part of the Song of Moses, which he recited before the children of Israel not long before his death; in this song, Moses reflects on God's faithfulness to an unfaithful people. In this portion of Moses's song, he shows the extent of God's faithfulness in protecting his people by comparing God's care to the powerful protection of an eagle over her young, saying, "As an eagle stirreth up her nest, fluttereth over her young, spreadeth abroad her wings, taketh them, beareth them on her wings: So the LORD alone did lead him, and there was no strange god with him." In other places in Scripture, God is compared to powerful animals to show the greatness of his power. In Hos 11:10, Hosea adds intensity to God's power by comparing him to a lion, saying, "They shall walk after the LORD: he shall roar like a lion: when he shall roar, then the children shall tremble from the west." Hosea shows his readers that Yahweh's voice alone can make even the strongest of nations tremble. So, in many places, the Bible uses a literary device called zoomorphism to intensify and make understandable God's attributes; Ps 91:4 is no exception.

So far, God has been described as a place of refuge, a fortress. Moses now describes God as a bird that protects his children under his wing. Moses began this verse using anthropomorphism to give humanlike qualities to God, explaining how he will cover those who are under his shadow; now Moses shifts to a zoomorphism, as seen in the remainder of the verse, to show God as a strong bird who pulls his children under his wing, offering them a place of refuge. Many commentators write that the wings that Moses refers to here actually describe the inmost feathers of God's wings, showing that he not only covers his children with his wings but pulls them close to his breast as he protects them. In *The Expositor's Bible Commentary*, a similar perspective is taken: "The 'wings' referred to here may represent the closest part of God's presence, symbolizing his protection and care, just as a bird uses its wings to shelter its young, keeping them close and safe."[7] As God uses the innermost part of his wing to hide his children, Moses emphasizes the intimacy of Yahweh's protection, showing his encompassing care for those who abide under his shadow. There is no safer place for a baby bird than beneath its mother's wings, close to her heart. Likewise, Moses describes those who abide in the shadow of the Almighty as dwelling in this place of ultimate protection. In this picture, Moses paints God protecting his children like a mother bird guarding her chicks; not only will these find refuge and security under the wings of Yahweh, being sheltered from the elements, but they will also find warmth and comfort. The promises of v. 4 add even more validity to Moses's claim in v. 1 that rest can be found under the shadow of the Almighty. For those who abide in the warmth and protection Yahweh provides under his wings, it will be these who will be able to finally rest comfortably from their enemies.

Moses once again shows Yahweh as a personal God to his people based on his actions in v. 4. God does not simply send his angels alone to offer protection, nor does he rely on those he has established in government, but God personally takes those who abide under his shadow and pulls them under his wings to blanket them with his loving protection. There is no safer place to be than under the wings of Yahweh. No bunker, building, or any amount of military protection can provide such a place of warmth and protection that Yahweh gives. Only those, as Moses has shown us earlier, who continually abide in the secret places of the Most High (v. 1) will experience this warmth and protection under the wings of Yahweh. Puritan preacher Thomas Watson says, "God's wings are a shield to defend us, a canopy to cover us, and a sanctuary to protect us."[8] Moses can attest to this, as he often experienced the protection of Yahweh while traveling from Egypt to Canaan. Matthew Henry states regarding Yahweh's protection: "He will

---

7. Gaebelein, *Expositor's Bible Commentary*, 594.
8. Watson, *Body of Divinity*, 271.

cover thee with his feathers and under his wings shalt thou turn, his truth shall be thy shield and buckler."[9] At the end of this verse, Moses validates Henry with these words: "His truth shall be thy shield and buckler."

THE PROVISION OF HIS PROTECTION (V. 4C)

It is under the wings of Yahweh, amid his protecting feathers, that Moses says one can take refuge. Moses then explains why these can take refuge in the latter part of v. 4, saying, "His truth shall by thy shield and buckler." In other words, not only will God's wings provide a place of refuge, but you can take refuge there, trusting in God's faithfulness. God's faithfulness is the real weapon that protects his people from their enemies. God is faithful in taking care of those who abide under his shadow, and as a God who never goes back on his promises, these can be sure that Yahweh will protect them at all costs if they continually abide with him. So, Yahweh's faithfulness in his truth is a shield and a buckler to those who abide in him. God is shown to be faithful to his promises throughout Scripture, so Moses's promises concerning what Yahweh will do to those who abide under his shadow are guaranteed. Therefore, those who abide in his shadow can take refuge in him, knowing he will do what he says he will do for his people.

God's sovereignty over his promises guarantees his faithfulness in keeping his promises. Many Scriptures attest to God's sovereignty over his plans and promises, showing that whatever God has promised to come to pass or to do, he will bring it to pass. One of the greatest attestations of God's sovereignty over his promises is seen in his words spoken through the mouth of Isaiah, saying:

> Remember this, and shew yourselves men: bring it again to mind, O ye transgressors. Remember the former things of old: for I am God, and there is none else; I am God, and there is none like me, Declaring the end from the beginning, and from ancient times the things that are not yet done, saying, My counsel shall stand, and I will

---

9. Henry, *Matthew Henry's Commentary*, 937.

> do all my pleasure: Calling a ravenous bird from the east, the man that executeth my counsel from a far country: yea, I have spoken it, I will also bring it to pass; I have purposed it, I will also do it. (Isa 46: 8–11)

In this passage, God reveals that he has already "declar[ed] [or ordained] the end from the beginning, and from ancient times the things that are not yet done," showing that all his promises and plans will come to pass because he has already ordained them to come to pass. So, in his sovereignty, not allowing one of his plans to be thwarted or overturned, God will bring to pass what Moses has promised here to those who abide under his shadow. Therefore, we can take refuge in Yahweh's faithfulness to his promises and to his word, trusting that all he has promised to those who abide under his shadow will come to pass. His faithfulness is his ultimate weapon that protects us from the Evil One.

Once again, Moses confirms in this passage that God is a place of refuge where those who abide in him can find protection. Not only is protection found under his wings, but protection is found in his faithfulness to his promises. You may tell yourself, "I have never experienced this type of refuge before, even though I know God is a place of refuge." You may wonder how you can finally take refuge in God, resting in him and trusting that he will protect you from the Evil One. Moses explains how one can find this place of refuge under the shadow of the Almighty. As Moses makes clear in v. 1, to find refuge in Yahweh, you must continually abide in him. In other words, to experience such a place of refuge, you must continually commune with Yahweh, delighting in his word, meditating on his word, worshiping him, and praying to him. The more you delight in his word and commune with him, the more you will learn about his attributes, such as his power and sovereignty. It is upon these truths that you will be able to find rest. Knowing that Yahweh is the Most High, meaning he is in complete control over all things, will provide you peace and comfort as you seek refuge in him. The more you abide in him, the more you will learn about his goodness and mercy, offering comfort and rest as you abide under his shadow. Therefore, the first step in taking refuge in Yahweh, trusting in his faithfulness, etc., begins with abiding with him, as Moses states in v. 1.

CONCLUSION

If there was ever a man who could attest to Yahweh being that wonderful place of refuge, it was Moses. However, Moses is not the only one who can attest to God being a place of refuge; powerful men like David call Yahweh his "refuge" many times throughout the Psalms. As David faced numerous dangers, persecutions from Saul, and many other heartaches, Yahweh proved to be faithful to David, allowing David to take refuge in him. God often proved faithful to David, delivering him from one atrocity after the other, showing that David could trust in him and take refuge in him. If God has kept you in any way throughout your life, then there is reason enough to continue to trust and take refuge in him.

The word "truth" or "faithfulness," depending on which translation you may be reading, describes Yahweh's power to keep his word for his people. The Greek version of the Old Testament, the Septuagint, renders this verse more clearly, saying, "His faithfulness is the weapon that surrounds you." In other words, God's faithfulness to his people in providing for them, protecting them, delivering them, and doing the many other things he has promised to his people is like a shield protecting you. God is faithful to those who abide in his shadow. Not only is God faithful in keeping the promises Moses has given us so far, but he is also faithful in keeping all his promises scattered throughout Scripture. Even in our unfaithfulness, God remains faithful, and it is in this promise we can take refuge.

So, what will you find under the shadow of the Almighty? You will find a place of refuge, because God himself will cover you with his wings and shield you with his faithfulness. Charles Spurgeon captures the beauty of Moses's promise concerning Yahweh's protection in this verse and offers us a good conclusion to this section of the book, saying:

"*His truth*"—his true promise, and his faithfulness to his promise "*shall be thy shield and buckler.*" Double armor has he who relies upon the Lord. He bears a shield and wears an all-surrounding coat of mail—such is the force of the word 'buckler.' To quench fiery darts, the truth is a most effectual shield, and to blunt all swords, it is an equally effectual coat of mail. To quench fiery darts, the truth is a most effectual shield, and to blunt all swords, it is an equally effectual coat of mail. Let us go forth to battle thus harnessed for the war, and we shall be safe in the thickest of the fight.[10]

---

10. Spurgeon, *Treasury of David* 3, 234. Emphasis original.

4

A Life Lived in the Absence of Fear

Psalm 91:5-10

INTRODUCTION

SO FAR, IN THE first few verses of Ps 91, Moses has painted a beautiful portrait of what life is like under the shadow of the Almighty. Life under the shadow of the Almighty is a sweet life of rest, a life marked by deliverance and protection, a life in which one can find refuge from the raging seas of life. In v. 1, Moses describes life under the shadow of the Almighty as a life where God provides a place of lodging where one can find rest from the elements, out of the rain, and out of the current storm that one may be facing. The type of verb Moses uses for the word "rest" or "lodging" is an imperfect verb, meaning that God provides a place of continual lodging and rest while abiding under his shadow. While lodging under his shadow, the promise of deliverance that Moses gives to those who abide there makes the lodging under God's shadow even more appealing. In vv. 2–3, Moses makes clear that this deliverance is a personal deliverance exclusively given by Yahweh God, showing his readers that no other being, including the false gods that many served during this time, can provide such a great deliverance.

To demonstrate the exclusiveness of Yahweh as our deliverer as we abide under his shadow, Moses uses the covenantal name of God when he says, "I will say to the Lord." By using the covenantal name of God, Moses is saying it is only the God of Israel, Yahweh God, whose shadow can provide such great deliverance. To emphasize his clarity of Yahweh God being the only one who can provide such a shadow of deliverance, he continues saying it is this Yahweh God who is "my refuge and my fortress; my God, in him I will trust." Using the third-person singular pronoun "he" continually to refer to Yahweh in v. 2, Moses shows that he is ascribing to Yahweh alone this great deliverance found under his shadow. In other words, no other shadow but Yahweh's can provide deliverance from the snare of the fowler, namely the traps of the Devil. This life of rest and deliverance can be found under no one else's shadow but, as Moses shows, is attributed to Yahweh's shadow exclusively. According to Moses, Yahweh's deliverance is all-encompassing, extending from protection against the fowler's snare to deliverance from raging pestilence and everything in between.

Not only is deliverance found under his shadow, but according to v. 4, protection is also found there. As Moses continues our tour under the shadow of the Almighty, he now describes those who abide under Yahweh's shadow as being protected like baby chicks living under their mother's wing. Protected, guarded, and kept from the enemy, baby chicks remain in continual safety under their mother's wing, and so are the ones, as Moses shows us here, who abide in the shadow of the Almighty. Like living under the wing of a mother bird, Yahweh's shadow provides those who abide under it a place of shelter, warmth, and a place of peace because Yahweh, like a mother bird, blankets you with his pinions, pulling you close to the inner part of his wing, giving you guaranteed refuge. Moses shows the personal, protective nature of Yahweh for those who abide under his shadow when he says in v. 4, "He shall cover thee with his feathers, and under his wings shalt thou trust:

his truth shall be thy shield and buckler." Moses uses indicative statements to confirm that those who continually abide in the "secret place of the Most High" will find refuge, as Yahweh covers them like a bird sheltering her young beneath her wings. In v. 4, Moses uses the third-person singular pronoun "he" to refer to Yahweh, emphasizing that rest, deliverance, and protection come exclusively from Yahweh alone to those who abide under his shadow. Moses's continual use of the third-person singular pronoun in referring to Yahweh highlights the uniqueness of Yahweh's actions in providing these blessings to those who continually abide with him.

The combination of rest, deliverance, and protection that Yahweh provides for those under his shadow allows for a life absent of fear, as mentioned by Moses in v. 5. Verse 5 gives the ultimate result of abiding in the shadow of the Almighty, namely that those who abide under his shadow will find a life absent of fear. Those who lodge under Yahweh's shadow will be given a life no longer dominated by fear nor riddled with anxiety due to Yahweh's work alone in the lives of those who abide with him. In the New Testament, Jesus also shows us that those who abide with Yahweh have no reason to fear anymore, saying in his Sermon on the Mount, "Take no thought for your life, what ye shall eat, or what ye shall drink; nor yet for your body, what ye shall put on" (Matt 6:25). Jesus shows that we can have lives absent of fear if we continually "seek . . . the kingdom of God, and his righteousness" (Matt 6:33). Jesus strengthens his argument that we can live our lives in the absence of fear by saying, "Behold the fowls of the air: for they sow not, neither do they reap, nor gather into barns; yet your heavenly Father feedeth them. Are ye not much better than they?" (Matt 6:26). He continues to show that if God takes care of the flowers of the field and so on, how much more will he take care of us who were made in his image? With his words "Take no thought for your life," Jesus also shows us that those who abide closely with Yahweh, seeking him and delighting in him, can have a life absent of fear and worry.

Often, we think that a life absent of fear is only achievable when we get to heaven; however, Moses shows us in this psalm that a life absent of fear is achievable in the present to those who abide under the shadow of the Almighty. Unfortunately, many never experience this life absent of fear because they do not, as Moses poses in v. 1, continually "abide in the secret places of the Most High." If one desires to have rest, deliverance, and protection that leads to a life absent of fear, they must continually abide with Yahweh; Moses shows that there is no other option for obtaining such a wonderful life under Yahweh's shadow.

Sadly, fear has taken the place of joy in the life of the Christian. Instead of the Christian experiencing the constant joy he is promised throughout Scripture because of his salvation in Christ, he may experience short spurts of joy, while fear becomes that friend that never seems to go away. Fear, unfortunately, has become an accepted part of the lives of believers who have every reason and resource not to live in fear. Both the Old and New Testaments exhort us constantly that there is only one who we are to fear, namely Yahweh, and it is exclusively Yahweh who can relieve our fears. As Scripture reveals—and Ps 91 is no exception—from the simplest of enemies to the government to the Evil One himself, Satan, there is no one but Yahweh that we should fear.

We must remember that Yahweh God, our Father, owns all things (Ps 24:1), and he is in ultimate control over all things, possessing complete sovereignty. In the first verse of this psalm, Moses emphasizes Yahweh's sovereignty, adding to the many reasons why we should not live in fear of anything if we are abiding with this sovereign God. Emphasizing Yahweh's sovereignty in v. 1, Moses ascribes to Yahweh two names: first, Yahweh is the Most High, and second, he is the Almighty. As the Most High and as the Almighty, Yahweh is sovereign over all things, including our bodies, our enemies, our birth, our death, our suffering, our tomorrows, and our next weeks; therefore, when we grasp the magnitude of Yahweh's sovereignty, particularly his sovereignty over our lives, we should no longer fear anything but him. In this psalm, Moses attempts to show us the many powerful actions of Yahweh over the lives of his people, revealing his strength and sovereignty, all with the hope of showing us that if we abide under Yahweh's shadow, only then can we truly live a life absent of fear.

A life lived in fear is debilitating; for the Christian, a life lived in fear is a life absent of fearing God. At the root of our fear is an absence of trusting Yahweh, which stems from not knowing him. Thankfully, Moses reminds us of who God is while showing us what life can be like if we abide under his shadow. Many great preachers of old speak on the debilitating effects of fear in the life of the Christian. Puritan John Owen says, "Fear is a Spirit that distresses and weakens the soul,"[1] while Charles Spurgeon says, "Anxiety does not empty tomorrow of its sorrows, but only empties today of its strength."[2] Both statements ring true for those who do not abide under the shadow of the Almighty. God must be the only one we are to fear if we desire a life absent of fear, and this fear of God shows itself in our continual abiding with him. Puritan Thomas Brooks confirms that a life absent of fear is lived in fear of Yahweh, saying, "He that fears God will fear nothing else."[3] Paul's words to Timothy highlight that Yahweh desires his people to live lives that are absent of fear, echoing Moses's assurance in Ps 91. In 2 Tim 1:7, Paul declares, "For God hath not given us the spirit of fear; but of power, and of love, and of a sound mind." Both Moses and Paul highlight God's provision of protection, strength, and peace to show that those who trust him have no reason to live in fear.

So, how do we get to a place where our lives are absent of fear? To live a life without fear, we must abide under the shadow of the Almighty, trusting in the promises that Moses makes concerning this life in the verses surrounding v. 5. Notice Moses makes a profound promise in v. 5, saying, "Thou shalt not be afraid." The location of this promise is key to understanding how to obtain it. This promise is tucked between v. 1 and vv. 9–10, which are connected in their exhortations to Moses's readers. Both v. 1 and

---

1. Owen, *Works of John Owen*, 81.
2. Spurgeon, *Salt-Cellars*, 12.
3. Brooks, *Heaven on Earth*, 77.

vv. 9–10 show us where a life absent of fear begins. Moses indicates in v. 1 that only those abiding in the "secret places of the Most High" will experience the promises given at the end of v. 1 through v. 4 that breed a life absent of fear. Verse 9 also shows the exclusiveness of those who will have a life absent of fear: "Thou hast made the Lord, which is my refuge, even the most High, thy habitation." Verse 10 provides even more reasoning as to why those who make Yahweh their place of habitation can live a life absent of fear; namely, "There shall no evil befall thee, neither shall any plague come nigh thy dwelling." Therefore, those who continually "abide in the secret places of the Most High" (v. 1) and those who make Yahweh their place of "habitation" (v. 9) will be those who will no longer live in fear (v. 5).

So, after fleshing out what God does for those who abide in his shadow in vv. 1–4, Moses now begins to tell us in vv. 5–10 the result of God's works in our lives as we abide in his shadow, namely a life absent of fear. Moses understood what it felt like to not live in fear after seeing God deliver him and his people many times as they made their way to the promised land. Due to his confidence in Yahweh, Moses alone encourages his people as they are on the verge of entering into the promised land not to be afraid, showing them why they can enter into the promised land in the absence of fear, saying, "Be strong and of a good courage, fear not, nor be afraid of them: for the Lord thy God, he it is that doth go with thee; he will not fail thee, nor forsake thee" (Deut 31:6).

Jesus, being not only fully man but fully God, also offers a similar promise that Moses gives, showing that he will be with his people to the end of the age, giving them reason not to live in fear after he is gone. As he commissions his disciples to go throughout the entire world to deliver the gospel, knowing they were afraid after seeing their Savior die on the cross, Jesus comforts them, giving them reason not to be frightened, showing them they have nothing to fear, saying "lo, I am with you always, even unto the end of the world" (Matt 28:20). In other words, dwelling in God's presence and trusting in his rest, his deliverance, and his protection, leads to a life absent of fear. So, here is a promise that seems impossible, that seems farfetched, that seems like a stretch: the word of God, through the mouth of Moses, promises that the one who abides in the shadow of the Almighty will experience a life absent of fear (v. 5). Moses begins in v. 5 to flesh out this promise of a life without fear; he shows us that this fearless life under God's shadow is first guaranteed.

A FEARLESS LIFE GUARANTEED (VV. 5-6)

An Exclusive Guarantee (v. 5a)

Moses begins with the pronoun "you," showing that this fearless life is exclusive only to "you," namely those abiding in the "secret places of the Most High," who will be found under the shadow of the Almighty. To these exclusively is given this promise of a life absent of fear. Immediately, Thus, not everyone will experience a life that is absent of fear. It's impossible to live without fear apart from knowing and trusting God; to know God, you must continually abide with him under his shadow. Without knowing God, even the mightiest of people fear; the smartest, the wealthiest, and the most confident of men and women fear. According to Moses, only those who know God by abiding in him under his shadow will be the ones who "shall not fear." Even more profoundly, this guarantee is exclusive not to every believer, but only to believers who continually commune and abide with their Father, who is in heaven.

Unfortunately, many believers live most of their lives in fear, just as they did before they came to Christ. Many aspects of their life may have changed, but their fear of the unknown, their fear of their enemies, and so on remained intact. If fear were the determining factor in identifying a Christian, many would be indistinguishable from unbelievers. Like the lost, many Christians fear for their lives, health, finances, future, and the unknown—ultimately because they do not abide in the Most High. Since they do not continually abide with God, they barely know him, only hearing about him through preaching and occasionally reading about him. It is those who barely commune with God that will live most of their Christian life in the sin of fearing not only God but everything else. God desires that we only fear him and nothing else. Christians are called to fear God alone, and that fear is generated through constant abiding in him. When Christians fear God entirely, they will not fear anything else because they know that God is completely sovereign over all things, including those who are their enemies. Since most Christians do not continually commune with him daily, not spending time with him through a life bathed with prayer and fellowship, many will not experience the rest, deliverance, and protection that Moses has spoken of in the previous verses; therefore, they will not experience a life that is absent of fear. However, for those who abide with God, living under his shadow, Moses does not simply say it is possible for you to no longer live in fear, but as an indicative statement, Moses declares as a guarantee that for those who are found under the shadow of the Almighty, "You shall not fear" (v. 5).

A Continual Guarantee (v. 5b)

The Hebrew verb for "fear" is negated at the beginning with the Hebrew particle usually translated as "not" attached to it, showing a chance of a life absent of fear for those who abide in Yahweh. However, to add even more incentive to abiding with Yahweh, it is not simply the absence of fear you will experience in your life but a continual absence of fear that will never cease as long as you are abiding under Yahweh's shadow. The Hebrew verb for "fear" is written as a Qal imperfect, denoting a potentially continual state of being and ending. In other words, life under the shadow of the Almighty provides a life of continual rest, deliverance, and protection, and, through these promises, a continual absence of fear.

Abiding with God offers not one moment of fear, but rather a continual state of fearing nothing except God. In the constant absence of fear, those who abide under God's shadow can live in a state of continuous peace. Therefore, those who continually abide in the secret places of the Most High will constantly live in the absence of fear. David echoes this truth in Ps 23 when he describes

Yahweh as a shepherd who leads his sheep through many stages of life, namely places of bliss "beside still waters" but also through the "valley of the shadow of death." Whether Yahweh's sheep are beside still waters or sojourning through the valley of the shadow of death, David says we will fear no evil because "thou art with me; thy rod and thy staff they comfort me." So, for those who continually abide with the great shepherd, Yahweh, you do not have to fear any part of your life, especially when walking through life's darkest valleys, including the valley of the shadow of death.

In the New Testament, Jesus offers exhortation to his disciples that they are not to fear and do not have to fear anything if they are continually seeking the kingdom of God and his righteousness. While giving the Sermon on the Mount, Jesus exhorts his listeners on how to live as citizens of the kingdom of heaven in a fallen world and says, "Take therefore no thought for the morrow" (Matt 6:34). Jesus is saying that as citizens of the kingdom of heaven, you no longer have to fear your tomorrow, namely anything concerning your life, "what ye shall eat, what ye shall drink; nor yet for your body," because if God has taken care of the least of his creation, he will take care of the greatest of his creation: his image bearers. As Jesus shows, for us who constantly seek first the kingdom of God and his righteousness, those who, in Moses's words, are "abiding in the secret places of the Most High," have no reason to fear because of God's unmatched provision.

God desires his children only to live life fearing him—nothing and no one else.[4] The fear that God calls us to is a reverential fear that reveals our trust in him. As Paul says, God has not given us the spirit of "timidity, but of power and love and discipline" (2 Tim 1:7, NASB 1995). The Greek word Paul uses here for "timidity" is the word *deilias*, which is used only once in the entire New Testament, meaning "timidity" or "cowardice." In other words, God does not desire his children to live in timidity or a constant state of worry; rather, he longs for us to revere him, which

---

4. Scripture references for God's call to fear only him are Deut 6:13; 10:12; 10:20; Josh 24:14; Prov 29:25; many other verses scattered throughout the Old and New Testaments.

brings us to a place where we do not have to be timid of anything. While we have times of fear and worry in our lives, the more we grow to fear God by abiding continually with him, the less we fear those things surrounding us. Indeed, one cannot both fear God and live in timidity of everything else. If one is living in a constant state of worry and timidity, then they are likely not communing with God regularly; thus, they are not abiding under the shadow of the Almighty.

We must constantly abide under his shadow if we are going to live a life free of fear. The longer you abide in him, the longer you experience his rest, experience his deliverance, and witness his protection, leading to a life without fear. The longer you abide under the shadow of the Almighty, the more you will become like Moses, who wrote this psalm, and you will be able to attest to the wonderful benefits that God offers those who abide under his shadow. You will be able to say like David—who at the end of his life declared without a doubt in many of his psalms that God would never leave nor forsake him—that God is doubtless his place of refuge, his fortress, and his bulwark continually, giving David every reason not to fear anything but Yahweh. To show his readers the depth and breadth of this fearless life that is found under Yahweh's shadow, Moses covers a broad range of things that God's shadow relieves us from. In covering a broad range of things that would strike fear in most, Moses shows us that from the greatest to the least of things that can cause us fear, we do not have to be afraid if we are abiding under the shadow of the Almighty.

Broadness of This Guarantee (vv. 5c–6)

By providing a broad stroke of things, Moses shows us that we no longer have to be afraid, that nothing in this world should strike fear in us while under the shadow of the Almighty. From the smallest to the greatest of things, no matter the time or the season, there is nothing to fear for those who abide under the shadow of the Almighty. Using words like "day," "night," "noonday," and "darkness," Moses shows us that in every season of our lives, at all times in our lives, there is no time in our lives where we should be afraid if we are abiding in the shadow of the Almighty. Moses continues to show the broadness of the protection God's shadow provides us so we do not have to live in fear. God's shadow offers us protection at all times and from all things, like terror, arrows, pestilence, and destruction. The examples that Moses gives in his list of things we are no longer to be afraid of are things that can kill and destroy the body of man, taking their lives. Even with these extreme things that may harm us, Moses shows us that Yahweh's shadow is mighty enough to protect us from them, relieving our fears.

In his description of things that may afflict us, Moses gives humanlike qualities to these enemies, showing the very real reality that there is always something lurking to take down those who follow God, but even so, we have no reason to be afraid. Even though the arrow flies, the pestilence walks, and the destruction wastes away, all their efforts to harm us will prove futile because we are covered and blanketed under the shadow of the Almighty. Interestingly, in this list, Moses denotes that both present and unexpected threats are no longer to be feared by those who abide under the shadow of the Almighty. By describing pestilence as an enemy who "walketh in the darkness" (*holek b'opel*), Moses suggests an unseen, creeping danger from this enemy; yet even so, this enemy remains powerless against those under God's shadow. Therefore, no matter the type of enemy, the time of day when the enemy may strike, or the enemy's intention, those who abide under God's shadow are protected from these enemies.

The list of things that may harm those who follow Yahweh is not exhaustive; the reader can add whatever fear they may have to this list or whatever person, place, or thing that may harm them. Hostile kings, presidents, mighty men, governmental systems, employers, slanderers, backbiters, or any type of enemy can be added to this list of things that the one who abides under the shadow of the Almighty no longer must fear. The common denominator of the list that Moses provides is that all these things that seek to destroy Yahweh's followers attempt to do so to the point of death. Death is one of man's greatest enemies and, therefore, one of humankind's greatest fears; however, even the potential of death that these enemies offer Yahweh's followers no longer needs to be feared if one is abiding under the shadow of the Almighty. Just as the apostle Paul says in the New Testament to the church in Corinth, for the Christian, death no longer has its sting; therefore, death is no longer to be feared. Paul emphasizes Christ's victory over death, thus giving those who are in him victory over death, also allowing them freedom from the fear of death. Paul, comforting the church at Corinth concerning death by reminding them of their victory in Christ, says, "O death, where is thy sting? O grave, where is thy victory? The sting of death is sin; and the strength of sin is the law. But thanks be to God, which giveth us the victory through our Lord Jesus Christ" (1 Cor 15:55–57). Therefore, for those who abide under the shadow of the Almighty, namely those in Christ, death is simply an afterthought; it has been conquered in Christ and, therefore, nothing to be feared any longer.

A FEARLESS LIFE SECURED (V. 7)

In v. 7, Moses says, "A thousand shall fall at thy side, and ten thousand at thy right hand; but it shall not come nigh thee"; those who dwell under the shadow of the Almighty can be sure that their enemies will get their due recompense. Moses shows us here that all our enemies will be recompensed by God in his timing, even the enemies of sin and death. Long after this psalm was written, Christ would destroy both sin and death by his cross and his resurrection, putting an end to the "handwriting of ordinances that was against us, which was contrary to us, and took it out of the way, nailing it to his cross" (Col 2:14). Christ would conquer other of our greatest enemies, namely Satan and his demons, through his cross as well, as Paul finishes his statement concerning the effect of Christ's passion on the cross in Col 2:15: "And having spoiled principalities and powers, he made a shew of them openly, triumphing over them in it." Christ would become our ultimate victory for those who abide in him; the victory that Christ obtained over the enemies of God also became our victory.

If there was ever anyone who witnessed their enemies falling one by one by the hand of God, it was Moses. After crossing the Red Sea on dry ground, Moses looked behind him to see one of the greatest defeats of the enemy that he ever witnessed. As he turned and looked behind him at what once was a dry path surrounded by water on both sides, he watched as Yahweh released the waters, allowing them to return to where they once stood, engulfing the Egyptian army that was attempting to make it through the Red Sea via the same path Moses had taken. God had used water again, this time on a much smaller scale, to destroy the enemy of him and his people. Moses's experience with Yahweh allows him to confidently make a promise here in Ps 91 of Yahweh's complete delivery of his people from the hands of their enemies, saying in v. 7, "A thousand shall fall at thy side, and ten thousand at thy right hand; but it shall not come nigh thee." The word for "ten thousand" would be better rendered "myriad," since the Hebrew word *elep* describes a number without a limit, perhaps to show that God is not limited as to how many of our enemies he can deliver us from. The countless enemies Yahweh has the power to deliver his people from are further confirmed with the verb "may fall" or *yippol*, which is an imperfect verb. As an imperfect verb, Moses is not saying there will be a one-time deliverance of ten thousand of your enemies or a one-time deliverance of a certain number of enemies but that God is going to continually deliver those who abide under his shadow from their enemies, so there is no set number Moses can place here on the number of enemies God will destroy. Thus, Moses uses the word *elep* correctly to show that each of us will be delivered from a different number of enemies, a number that cannot be nailed down. The Greek Septuagint's rendering of the word "ten thousand" also shows that Moses speaks of a number without limit, which may vary from person to person. The word used for "ten thousand" in the Septuagint's translation of Ps 91:7 is the word *murioi*, which means "a countless number," so the passage really states that a numberless number of enemies will fall at your right hand. No matter the case, Moses is saying not only do you not have to worry about the terror of the night, nor the arrow that flies by day, nor the pestilence that stalks in darkness, nor the destruction that wastes at noonday, but you also do not need to worry about your enemies. The many things that may attempt to harm you, including your enemies, no matter their number, all will fall at your right hand and will not come near to you, Moses says, giving yet another reason why those who abide under Yahweh's shadow can have a life absent of fear.

Many times in Scripture, we've seen where God has intervened on behalf of those who abide with him, confirming Moses's promises that Yahweh will continue to intervene for those who abide under his shadow. In Gen 14:20, after Melchizedek blesses Abraham, he makes sure to bless Yahweh for his work in Abraham's life, explicitly delivering Abraham from his enemies. Melchizedek says to Abraham in Gen 14:20, "And blessed be the most high God, which hath delivered thine enemies into thy hand." Abraham is not the only one who saw God deliver him from his enemies one by one; others throughout Scripture would be able to give testimony of God's faithful work in delivering them from their enemies as they watched him do so before their very eyes. For example, in Exod 14, Moses, after watching God move in a mighty way, striking plague after plague upon Egypt, confidently tells the Israelites, who were afraid they were going to die due to the countless Egyptians trailing them and seeking their lives as the Israelites departed from Egypt, that "the LORD shall fight for you, and ye shall hold your peace." Moses understood that God had the power to deliver his people from their enemies, so Moses comforted his people many times, telling them that Yahweh would deliver them. In the next chapter, namely Exod 15:3, Moses boldly states regarding God's delivering power that "the LORD is a man of war: the LORD is his name." As a man of war, God knows how to fight for his people, deliver his people, and abolish the enemies of his people. Later, God shows himself to be their greatest deliverer who personally intervenes on his people's behalf, saying to Moses, "I will send my fear before thee, and will destroy all the people to whom thou shalt come, and I will make all thine enemies turn their backs unto thee" (Exod 23:27). God's sovereign rule over the enemies of his people is seen in this verse as well as the following few verses in Exod 23, where God promises to personally "drive out" many of their enemies, namely the Hivites, the Jebusites, and so on. Many times, Scripture shows that God brings complete control over the enemies of his people by either giving them into the hands of his people or giving his people into their hands to bring chastisement upon them. Not only does Moses give testimony of God's deliverance of him from his enemies, but King David later will have his fair share of enemies who will come up against him, and it will be each one that David will watch fall at the hand of Yahweh.

Like Moses's testimony of God's delivering power from the enemy in Ps 91, David recalls in many of the psalms where God has vindicated him from his enemies. Particularly in Ps 9:3, David uses another word to describe God's actions toward David's enemies. David says that not only will the Lord cause the enemy to stumble, but they will also perish away. David's confidence in his God bleeds out in Ps 9, especially in v. 3, where David begins his statement not with the word "if" but "when": "When mine enemies are turned back, they shall fall and perish at thy presence." David knows, without a shadow of a doubt, that Yahweh will vindicate him from his enemies, as should we who abide under the shadow of the Almighty. Although a different Hebrew word for "fall" is used in Ps 91:7 compared to Ps 9:3, the concept of the enemies of God's people falling at the hands of the Almighty is the same. In Judg 5, Deborah's song describes the victory of Jael over Sisera, the enemy of God's people; she sings of how Jael thrust a tent peg into the temple of Sisera and then describes his death by using the word "fall" multiple times. A portion of Deborah's song goes as follows in Judg 5:27: "At her feet he bowed, he fell, he lay down: at her feet he bowed, he fell: where he bowed, there he fell down dead." The enemy of God's people, the wicked Sisera, fell by the hand of God through Jael's bravery.

In most cases, God not only blesses his people by vindicating them from their enemies but he blesses them also by allowing them to see his work in eradicating their enemies. God desires his name to be praised above all others and will not share his glory with any created thing—especially in matters of our deliverance. Therefore, at times, he allows us to witness his deliverance firsthand so that we may give him alone the credit and praise he deserves. Thus, Moses promises just that in v. 8, namely that those who abide under the shadow of the Almighty will not have to do anything to deliver themselves from their enemy but watch as Yahweh does all the work. Moses says in v. 8, "Only with thine eyes shalt thou behold and see the reward of the wicked." Under the shadow of the Almighty, we will not only get the pleasure of knowing that our enemies are defeated, but we will also get the pleasure of seeing Yahweh work in defeating our enemies. In other words, Yahweh does not require us to help him when he delivers us from our enemies; all he desires us to do is watch as they fall.

Simply watching from the sidelines as God overtakes your enemies takes great faith. It is easy to take matters into our own hands, attempting by our strength to vindicate ourselves from our enemies; however, Moses teaches us through this promise to sit back and watch the salvation of Yahweh, which is exactly what Moses called his people to do as Yahweh delivered them from the Egyptians—taking us back again to that day when Moses and the sons of Israel gazed upon a vast wall of water in front of them, the Red Sea, while a raging army of angry Egyptians was behind them. Neither Moses nor his people could do anything at that moment; they could only watch and see if God was going to deliver them. As many folks began to panic about not having anywhere to go as their enemy drew closer—God putting them in a corner, if you will, so they would have to rely upon him—Moses chimes in with some comforting words, saying, "Fear ye not, stand still, and see the salvation of the LORD, which he will shew you to day: for the Egyptians whom ye have seen to day, ye shall see them again no more for ever" (Exod 14:13). These who had a wall of sea in front of them and an Egyptian army closing behind them had no other choice but watch as Yahweh delivered them from their enemies. Moses is telling us that we are to do the same: simply watch as God delivers us from the enemy, not taking matters into our own hands. Paul echoes this concept in Rom 12:19 as he is explaining to his listener what a life that has been offered to God as a living sacrifice looks like: "Dearly beloved, avenge not yourselves, but rather give place unto wrath: for it is written, Vengeance is mine; I will repay, saith the Lord." With these words, Paul exhorts his readers as followers of Christ to show that they are not to seek vengeance upon their enemies but trust that God will give them their due recompense. With these comforting words by Moses in Ps 91:8, for those who abide under the shadow of the Almighty, you no longer have to fight, you no longer have to plan accordingly based on what might happen to you from your enemies; simply rest and watch as God delivers you from them.

THE CONDITIONALITY OF THIS FEARLESS LIFE (VV. 9-10)

In vv. 9-10, Moses nails down again, as he did back in v. 1, the idea that a life under the shadow of the Almighty is conditional; therefore, a life absent of fear is conditional. Verse 1 and vv. 9-10 work in sync to show the exclusiveness of those who will experience these promises Moses has detailed for those who abide under the shadow of the Almighty; both verses 1 and 9-10 are statements of fact indicating that there are no alternatives as to who will obtain these precious promises that stem from a life lived under the shadow of the Almighty. The first condition Moses gives as the only means to have a life under the shadow of the Almighty is found in v. 1, where he says it will be only those who "continually abide in the secret place of the Most High" (my translation) that will find themselves under the shadow of the Almighty. Verse 9 makes the condition even more personal when it says that the only reason why you can experience a life of rest, a life of deliverance, a life of protection, and a life absent of fear as you watch your enemies fall one by one is "because thou hast made the LORD, which is my refuge, even the most High, thy habitation [dwelling place]" (Ps 91:9). So this life under the shadow of the Almighty that promises the vindication of our enemies is exclusive only to those who continually abide in the secret places of the Most High

(v. 1) and have made the Most High their dwelling place or refuge (v. 9). Both conditions denote a constant abiding in Yahweh, which brings about the promises that Moses has given throughout this psalm. So, it is very clear that the only way one can experience a blessed life under the shadow of the Almighty is if they are constantly abiding with him. These statements, as indicative statements, mean there are no alternatives and no other options; one must abide continually with Yahweh, making him their dwelling place to experience life under the shadow of the Almighty.

Moses makes sure, in v. 9, that his listeners know that only Yahweh is to be their dwelling place or habitation if they want to experience this life without fear. In v. 9, he uses three different names of the Lord, including his covenantal name, Yahweh, to make sure no one doubts who they should abide in if they want to obtain these precious promises. Moses calls God Yahweh in the first part of v. 9, and then Moses gives God's name that Moses uses for him in v. 2, namely his "refuge." Moses also uses the name "Most High" to emphasize that this God alone provides such a sweet life under his shadow if you abide in him alone and make him alone your habitation. Therefore, only those who make this God their habitation will experience the type of life that Moses has described so far, which is only found under the shadow of the Almighty.

Verse 10 gives a reassuring statement in the way of a promise that summarizes what those who have made Yahweh their "habitation" will experience, namely that for those who have done so, "there shall no evil befall thee, neither shall any plague come nigh thy dwelling." Using the words "evil" and "plague," Moses gives a range of enemies of God that includes every enemy that Yahweh will not allow to befall those who abide under his shadow. So why can only those who abide under the shadow of the Almighty live a life absent of fear? Verse 10 answers this question by summarizing everything Moses has said so far, saying that for those who abide under the shadow of the Almighty, "no evil will befall thee," and no plague will "come nigh" to their dwelling.

CONCLUSION

Puritan Thomas Watson once said, "He that hath God for his portion is above the fear of any danger, he need fear no loss for he hath the God of all, no affliction, for his God is his joy, no enemy, for God is his defense, no death, for God is his portion forever."[5] Psalm 91 resonates with Watson's claim in this quote, namely that those who abide in Yahweh need not fear anything or anyone but Yahweh alone. With a promised life absent of fear, there is no sweeter place to be than under the shadow of the Almighty. Moses makes it emphatically clear that only those who abide—dwelling, sitting, and remaining—with the Most High, the Almighty, Yahweh alone, will experience the blessings of his shadow. Verses 1–10 can be summed up this way: "Blessed is the one who abides in the shadow of the Almighty, for there he will no longer live in fear. For those who have tasted what life is like under the shadow of the Almighty, why not remain under his shadow to continue to experience a life marked by his provision? For those who want to experience what Moses has promised so far continually, regarding life under the shadow of the Almighty, don't just pull over for a moment under Yahweh's shadow, but live there, abide there, and settle under the wings of the Highest. It is there, in his shadow, that you will find a life free from fear.

---

5. Watson, *Divine Cordial*, 64.

5

A Life Preserved
Psalm 91:11–13

INTRODUCTION

ONE OF THE MOST extraordinary acts of God in his salvation for his people is his preservation of his people. One of the greatest spiritual truths that offers rest to the believer, provides security for the believer, and gives assurance to the believer is that God preserves those who are his. God's preserving power is seen early in the book of Genesis in creation, where God creates in such an order that each creation sustains the next. The creation of the garden of Eden reveals God's compassion in his provision and preservation of life due to his design of the garden, which provided all that was needed for survival. The garden was designed in such a way that it offered sustenance and nurturing to its inhabitants, reflecting his care for his creation. A fitting verse to support this provision is Gen 2:8–9 (ESV): "And the LORD God planted a garden in Eden, in the east, and there he put the man whom he had formed. And out of the ground the LORD God made to spring up every tree that is pleasant to the sight and good for food." The

Hebrew of these verses shows that God exclusively and personally implements his creation in such a way that offers provision and sustenance to his other creation. In these verses, we see that God personally planted plants and herbs in the garden to provide food to sustain his creation that would abide there. The Hebrew word *vayyitaa*, "and he planted," found in v. 8, is in the Qal imperfect, indicating a personal action by God. God did not use another creation to do his bidding in providing sustenance to those who would dwell in the garden, but God himself instead intervened in his creation's preservation. Notably, God's most prized creation was placed in this garden to sustain them. The Hebrew word used to show that God personally placed man in a place of preservation is the word *wayyasem*—"and he put"— found in v. 8, denotes an intentional placement of this creation in the garden of Eden. To assure that his most prized creation, namely humankind, would be preserved, God himself caused the plants to grow in the garden of Eden, ensuring that his creation was sustained entirely by his provision alone. Man's efforts played no role in the garden's fruitfulness; every aspect of their preservation directly resulted from God's sovereign care, demonstrating that life and sustenance flow entirely from him.

These two verses in Gen 2 paint a beautiful picture of God's work in our salvation. Just as God alone both planted and grew the plants in the garden of Eden, ensuring the preservation of his creation by his provision alone, so in our salvation, every aspect of our being born again into a new creature, including our preservation as saints of God, flows entirely from God alone. Just as God sprang forth new life and implemented what was necessary to preserve it, similarly, in salvation, God alone brings forth a new creature, giving it a new heart, granting it faith to believe in Christ, and brings about its preservation through this faith. Just as the first man and woman were placed in an environment that would sustain them, believers are placed in Christ, where Christ alone preserves those given to him (John 6:39–40; 10:36–30). All of God's saving and preserving work is done by him alone, including the giving of our faith as the very thing that preserves us. In his letter to the Ephesians, Paul confirms God's giving of faith to those in Christ. In Eph 2:8–9, Paul says, "For by grace are ye saved through faith; and that not of yourselves: it is the gift of God: Not of works, lest any man should boast." It is this same faith that Peter says God uses to preserve those who he himself has caused to be born again (1 Pet 1:1–5). Therefore, God not only creates but sustains those he has created, making God the source of his creations' preservation.

Noah also would experience God's preserving power as God alone closed the door on the ark, keeping Noah and his family safe and secure, before he struck the earth with a cataclysmic flood. The same waters that God would use to judge the world would be the same waters in which he would bring Noah and his family to safety, preserving them from the judgment. So, in a sense, God used his judgment to safeguard those who had faith in him from his judgment, which is a small picture of what he did when he placed his judgment on Christ. Noah experienced God's preservation and many others, pointing to the ultimate preservation of his saints through Christ. God, through his grace, preserves Lot and his family by sending angels to evacuate them out of the wicked city of Sodom before God rains down fire and brimstone, destroying all who were left in that city. God's preservation is also seen in the lives of King David and many others throughout the remainder of Scripture. King David speaks of God's physical preservation repeatedly throughout the Psalms, giving testimony time and time again of God's protection of him from his enemies. Psalm 16 shows David's crying out to God for preservation in one of David's many battles with either Goliath, Saul, Absalom, or other enemies. David understood that God was the only one who could preserve him in his distress. Psalm 16 records David's plea to God: "Preserve me, O god: for in thee do I put my trust" (Ps 16:1). In many other psalms, David describes God as a bulwark, a fortress, a place of refuge, showing that the presence of God is a place of preservation, a place of security from the enemy.

David also speaks many times of God's preservation of his soul even when David falls or stumbles, spiritually speaking, demonstrating God's preserving power over the souls of his creation.

Of his fall into sin with Bathsheba and God's grace in sustaining him through that sinful episode, David says in Ps 37:23–24, "The steps of a man are established by the Lord, when he delights in his way; though he fall, he shall not be cast headlong, for the Lord upholds his hand" (ESV). In another psalm, David says, "When I thought, 'My foot slips,' your steadfast love, O Lord, held me up. When the cares of my heart are many, your consolations cheer my soul" (Ps 94:18–19, ESV). Repeatedly, David emphasizes his stumbling in some of his psalms, while also emphasizing Yahweh's grace in never abandoning him when he did stumble.

God's preserving power is seen in many other places in the Old and New Testaments. On a more corporate level, the Bible shows God's works in keeping and preserving his chosen people, Israel. From the time spent in the iron furnace of Egypt; through their wilderness journey; through their conquest in Canaan; through one wicked king after another; to their time spent under the heavy hand of oppressive nations such as Assyria, Babylon, Medo-Persia, Greece, and Rome; and even through today's turbulent times in Israel, God has never abandoned his people, Israel, but has sustained them every step of the way.

Even when Israel was not faithful to God, God was faithful to them through his covenant with Abraham. In his covenant with Abraham, Yahweh promised to provide protection and preservation to Abraham and his descendants, bringing about his promise that Abraham's seed would become a great nation. This preservation would be necessary as God continued to sustain Abraham's seed so that one day, through this line, his only begotten Son would be born, who would bless the entire earth (Gen 22:18). God throughout Scripture reminds Israel of his promise to preserve Abraham's seed and fulfills his promise of bringing from Abraham a seed that would bless the nations. In Isa 49:14–16, God reminds his people of this promise, comforting them by saying, "But Zion said, The Lord hath forsaken me, and my Lord hath forgotten me. Can a woman forget her sucking child, that she should not have compassion on the son of her womb? yea, they may forget, yet will I not forget thee. Behold, I have graven thee upon the palms of my hands; thy walls are continually before me." He goes on promising to continue keeping them from their enemies, saying in Isa 49:25-26, "But thus says the LORD, Even the captives of the mighty shall be taken away, and the prey of the terrible shall be delivered: for I will contend with him that contendeth with thee, and I will save thy children. And I will feed them that oppress thee with their own flesh; and they shall be drunken with their own blood, as with sweet wine: and all flesh shall know that I the LORD am thy Saviour and thy Redeemer, the mighty One of Jacob." If God were to lose Israel, if he were to turn away from Israel and let the enemy devour them because of their sins, then God would not receive the glory as being known as Redeemer, as Savior, as the mighty One of Jacob, so God must preserve his people for his name's sake, and to show that his will to keep his people will not be thwarted.

God shows his preservation of Israel throughout history by not only destroying the enemies of Israel by fighting for Israel, but also by changing Israel's heart never to turn away from him again. Thus, he works through external means to preserve his people, namely ridding them of their enemies, while also working through internal means such as changing their hearts, to bring about their preservation. God says in Jer 32:40, "And I will make an everlasting covenant with them, that I will not turn away from them, to do them good; but I will put my fear in their hearts, and they shall not depart from me." God does the same in our salvation. God not only works through outside means to preserve his people like the teaching of God's word, the fellowship with the saints, and the delivery from the Evil One, but God also works within the person to preserve them by changing their hearts (Ezek 11:19; 36:26), giving them faith (Eph 2:8-9), and even granting them the ability to repent of sins (2 Tim 2:25). Even Paul is confident of God's preserving power of those who are his in Christ when he says in Phil 1:6 "being confident of this very thing, that he which hath begun a good work in you will perform it until the day of Jesus Christ," the antecedent being their "fellowship in the gospel" (v. 5). Other places within the Old Testament show God's more personal preservation of his people on a more individual level. The first psalm of the Psalter alludes to those who continually abide in God's word and shun evil as those whom God will spiritually preserve. Those whom God has changed in their hearts to no longer abide in sin but abide in him, meditating on his word, will be like a "tree planted by the rivers of water, that brings forth his fruit in his season; his leaf also shall not wither; and whatsoever he doeth shall prosper." It is the power of God that preserves those who abide in his word.

Many other places show God's different means of preserving his people. David shows in his doxology of God's word in Ps 119:50 that God uses his word to preserve his people, saying, "This is my comfort in my affliction: for thy word hath quickened me." Solomon also makes promises concerning God's preserving power through his word in Prov 2:8, saying that through the wisdom that comes from the mouth of Yahweh, "He keepeth the paths of judgment, and preserveth the way of his saints." In vv. 10–11, Solomon continues with his admonishing of God's preserving power through his word, saying, "When wisdom entereth into thine heart, and knowledge is pleasant unto thy soul; Discretion shall preserve thee, understanding shall keep thee." He goes on to say that this wisdom that comes from the mouth of God ultimately preserves those to whom he gives it to by delivering them "from the way of the evil man" (v. 12) and from "the strange woman" (v. 16). In other words, the wisdom that God gives to those who fear him, as shown in chapter 1 of Proverbs, is the wisdom that will bring discernment into the person's life and preserve them.

Scripture repeatedly confirms that the entire Godhead works in tandem to preserve those they have saved. The promise of eternal life shows that God preserves those to whom he gives eternal life. The very definition of "eternal life" describes a life that will never end but that will continue into eternity. Who has the power to sustain life to make it eternal? Who has the power to give this eternal life? Only the One who himself has no beginning nor end, namely Yahweh God, who is self-existent. Therefore, it is God alone who gives eternal life and preserves those who are his.

Jesus alludes to our eternal life in an argument with the Pharisees, who did not believe Jesus was who he said he was. He explained their unbelief to them and why they remained in their unbelief, namely because they were not of his sheep, while also showing them what would happen to those who believe in him. Jesus says in John 10:27–28, "My sheep hear my voice, and I know them, and they follow me: And I give unto them eternal life; and they shall never perish, neither shall any man pluck them out of my hand." He goes on to show in the next verse that God the Father even works in their preservation as his sheep, saying in v. 29, "My Father, which gave them me, is greater than all; and no man is able to pluck them out of my Father's hand." He further confirms the Godhead's work in preserving his saints by saying in v. 30 that "I and my Father are one." So, God the Son preserves our lives, but the Father also does so in sync with his Son, since both are one.

Paul also reveals how the Godhead works in the preservation of the saints. In his letter to the Ephesians, Paul shows how the third person of the Trinity, the Holy Spirit, preserves his people, saying in Eph 1:13–14, "In whom ye also trusted, after that ye heard the word of truth, the gospel of your salvation: in whom also after that ye believed, ye were sealed with that Holy Spirit of promise, Which is the earnest [down payment] of our inheritance until the redemption of the purchased possession, unto the praise of his glory." It is God the Son who Paul says in 1 Cor 1:8 "shall also confirm you unto the end, that ye may be blameless in the day of our Lord Jesus Christ." In his letter to the Philippians, Paul, speaking of God the Father, shows that God will finish the work that he started within those in whom he has saved. Paul refers to God the Father in Phil 1:6 when he says, "Being confident of this very thing, that he which hath begun a good work in you will perform it until the day of Jesus Christ." The Father's work within those he has saved is further mentioned in the next chapter of Paul's letter to the Philippians, where Paul speaks of the believer's sanctification and shows that God alone ultimately works his will within our salvation. After Paul gives that famous command in Phil 2:12 to "work out your own salvation with fear and trembling," he then shows that it is ultimately God who works through us to carry out his will in by saying in the next verse, "For it is God which worketh in you both to will and to do of his good pleasure." So, the entire process of the believer's salvation, from the beginning to the end, is wrought by God alone. This is why he alone is credited with the preservation of his saints.

Another confirmation of God's preserving power to keep those whom he has saved is seen in the very words of God the Son. Jesus speaks of his work in keeping those whom the Father has given him in John 6:39–40: "And this is the Father's will which hath sent me, that of all which he hath given me I should lose nothing, but should raise it up again at the last day. And this is the will of him that sent me, that every one which seeth the Son, and believeth on him, may have everlasting life: and I will raise him up at the last day." Not one aspect of the Father's will will Jesus not accomplish, but everything the Father willed for his Son to do will be done, including losing none that the Father has given him but raising them all in the last day. If Jesus loses one, he has not fulfilled all the Father's will, thus severing himself from the remainder of the Godhead, who all have one will. If the Son did not obey his Father's will, then the Son would have fallen short and sinned against the Father, which Jesus did not and will not do; thus all that the Father has given him, he will carry out the Father's will in keeping them and raising them all in the last day, showing his preserving power as God over those who are his.

If there was anyone who experienced God's preserving power and understood its magnitude, it was Moses. Moses was the recipient of God's preserving power early in life. As a new pharaoh arose in Egypt who did not favor the Israelites, the Israelites would become a target, specifically the males, because this new pharaoh grew worried that if they continued to multiply, they would one day take over Egypt. To counter this potential threat of a hostile takeover by Israel, he ordered the Egyptian midwives of the Hebrew women to kill all the male children that were born to them, slowing down the population growth of the Israelites. Moses would be born not long after this order was given. However, Moses would not be on the receiving end of this order because God would preserve his life. God's sovereignty is seen not only in Moses's preservation but also in *how* he brings about Moses's preservation by stirring the heart of Moses's mother. Moses's mother placed him in an ark of bulrushes that she had woven so that he could be put into the river to float away to safety. In God's providence, the daughter of Pharaoh came down to wash herself at the river while her maidens walked along the river's edge. To her surprise, she saw the ark that Moses was in, and she flagged her maidens to fetch him. Through God's hand of preservation, Moses would be found and placed in the house of Pharaoh to be preserved at the care of his daughter. God preserved Moses so that one day, God could have an inside man in Egypt to be used in delivering his people from Egyptian bondage. In a sense, God would preserve Moses to bring about the preservation of his people in their eventual deliverance from Egypt.

This would not be the last time Moses experienced the preserving power of God. At a much older age, Moses witnessed God's preserving power repeatedly. Moses would witness God preserving him and his people from Pharaoh and Pharaoh's army as God opened the Red Sea for them to cross safely, then overthrowing the Egyptians in the Sea. Throughout his desert journey, Moses and the children of Israel would behold God's preserving work as he provided them with food, shelter, direction, and other means to bring them into the promised land. Moses attests to these acts of God's preservation in his writings, such as Exodus and Deuteronomy. Psalm 91 is no exception; in vv. 11–13, Moses again gives an account of God's preserving power when he promises preservation to those who abide under the shadow of the Almighty.

THE SOURCE OF OUR PRESERVATION (V. 11A)

Moses begins v. 11 with a subordinate conjunction, *ki*, connecting this verse to the previous verse. Verse 11 gives more detail as to how the promise presented in v. 10 will come about, namely the promise that "there shall no evil befall thee, neither shall any plague come nigh thy dwelling." Using the subordinate conjunction *ki*, translated as either "because" or "for," Moses says that evil will not befall you or any plague come near to you, "because" or "for" "he shall give his angels charge over thee, to keep thee in all thy ways." In other words, for those who abide in the secret places of the Most High, who find themselves dwelling under the shadow of the Almighty, God will sustain and preserve them not only through keeping them under his pinions but also by sending his angels to guard or keep them in all of their ways. Interestingly, the promise found in v. 10, namely that "no evil shall befall thee," is nestled between Moses's assurance that Yahweh will cover them with his wings, delivering them from their enemies (vv. 4–8), and Moses's assurance that he will send his angels to keep them (v. 11). Thus, God, in his grace and mercy, provides multiple layers of protection and preservation to those who abide under his shadow.

So as not to place too much emphasis on angels' or humankind's ability to preserve themselves, Moses shows that the source of these angels that are sent to protect those who abide under the shadow of the Almighty is Yahweh. The word for "his angels" is the Hebrew word *mal'ākāyw*. The way the word *mal'ākāyw* is written shows that it is possessive in nature, meaning that these angels belong to and are under the authority of Yahweh. The possessive nature of *mal'ākāyw* is indicated by the pronominal suffix *ayw*, a third-person masculine singular possessive suffix, meaning "his" or "belonging to him." When attached to the plural noun for "angels," this pronominal suffix makes the noun a construct with possession, meaning "his angels." Just as God planted and caused to grow the plants in the garden of Eden to preserve his creation, God personally created and sends his angels when necessary to preserve and protect his creation. In other words, without God being the initiator of our preservation, our preservation would never happen. Every act of preservation that has taken place in Scripture ultimately begins with God. The entire universe is preserved and sustained by him alone; thus, on a more individual level, God initiates the preservation of his people through whatever means he wills to do so, including the use of angels.

Moses, as before, uses the third-person singular to show that God alone sends his angels to our aid because it is God alone who has the authority to do so. Moses says, "For he shall give his angels charge over thee." By using the pronoun "he," Moses draws his readers back to the preceding verses, highlighting that it is this God, "the Most High," "the Almighty," and the many other names that Moses has used to refer to Yahweh, that alone controls the angelic armies of heaven, summoning them to do his bidding whenever he pleases. Since Yahweh is the one who created the angels, they are subject to him to do his bidding, and one of those biddings is to guard and keep those who are his. Moses comforts his readers by showing that God uses the strongest of his creations to watch over his prized creation, humankind. No creation is stronger and superior to that of God's angels, especially in their abilities. Thus, kings, princes, presidents, and so on cannot offer the protection and preservation that God's angels can for his people. So, for such a superior creation, only God, who is commander in chief over all creation, can summon these angelic beings to do his bidding in preserving those who abide under his shadow. Humankind can never accredit themselves nor anyone else in their preservation, because even kings, princes, presidents, and other dignitaries do not have the authority to call down from heaven such a mighty creation to preserve God's people. Only God has the authority to do so.

It is easy to see why Moses says it is this God he places his trust in back in v. 3, knowing that God has the power to dispatch countless angels to Moses's rescue whenever he pleases. The word Moses uses to describe God's command to his angels to keep his people shows the depth of his desire to preserve his people. Moses says, "He will give his angels charge or command concerning you" (my translation). In other words, due to God's desire to preserve his people, he commands his angels concerning his people, not insisting or begging, showing God's urgency concerning his people. As his creation, his angels must obey his voice in this matter. This means his angels have no option in guarding his people, but they must guard you at his command. Moses promises these angels will guard God's people, which is comforting news to those who abide under God's shadow.

Knowing that God's angels will obey his command to keep his people, Moses promises that those under God's shadow will be on the receiving end of God's preservation. These, under God's shadow, can rest knowing God is guarding them with his angels. They can also live in the absence of fear, as Moses mentions in v. 5, because those who abide under the shadow of the Almighty know that God himself not only is covering them with his wings and taking down their enemies (vv. 4–8) but that he has charged his angels concerning them as well (v. 11). The command that Yahweh issues to his angels in v. 11 to keep those abiding under his shadow is serious. The word for "command" comes from the Hebrew word *yĕtsawwê*, the root of which means to "command, order, appoint, or charge."[1] The verb *yĕtsawwê* is seen in many Old Testament passages, especially in passages where God gives authoritative commands to individuals, nations, and so on. *Yĕtsawwê* is used when God commands Adam to keep the garden in which he placed him, according to Gen 2:16. It is also the same verb used in Gen 6:22, where God commands Noah to build an ark to keep his family safe from the judgment to come. In other words, God's command to his angels concerning his people has no alternatives; these angels must guard those to whom God sends them, namely those abiding under the shadow of the Almighty. Thus, God is the ultimate source of our guarding because he is the sender of those who will guard us, we who abide under his shadow.

God is the "commander in chief" over all angelic beings. His authority over angels is seen in one of his titles ascribed to him throughout Scripture. In Scripture, God is often called the "Lord of hosts" or "Lord of armies," pointing to the vast army of angels that he commands. Moses's promise that Yahweh will dispatch his angels to keep those who are under his shadow is given precedent in other places in Scripture as well. While God is the source of his people's preservation, his angels are the agents he sometimes uses to carry out that preservation. Early in the chapters of Genesis, after Adam fell into sin within the garden that God had placed him in to be preserved, God, in his authority, sends an angel to

---

1. Brown et al., *Brown-Driver-Briggs*, 845.

keep guard over the garden of Eden after driving Adam and Eve out due to their sin. The account of God sending an angel to guard his garden of Eden is seen in Gen 3:24, which records that God appointed "Cherubims, and a flaming sword which turned every way, to keep the way of the tree of life." This would not be the last time God would use angels to do his bidding; later in Gen 19, God sends angels to evacuate Lot and his family from Sodom before inflicting harsh judgment on that unfaithful city, destroying it with fire and brimstone. So, the Bible attests in many places that God is in complete control over his angelic beings and will summon them to do his bidding whenever he wishes. Therefore, God alone must be credited with preserving those who abide under his shadow.

THE AGENTS OF OUR PRESERVATION (V. 11B)

Our preservation is so important to God that he does not rely upon us to preserve ourselves, but he, through various means, including the use of a much higher creation like angels, works to preserve his people. Notice that God does not give charge to kings or other dignitaries who are in some type of power to keep his people. Instead, God delegates this command of preserving his people to a much higher creation, namely his angels, who are able to guard and protect God's people from the most wicked of enemies, including the Evil One, Satan. It would be these angels who would minister to Christ after his grueling temptation from Satan in Matt 4:11. Thankfully, according to Moses in Ps 91:11–13, just as God sent his angels to minister to his Son, one of their greatest acts is the preservation of those who abide under the shadow of the Almighty. It is comforting to know that God gives those directly under him, namely his angelic beings, the duty to watch over his most prized possession, namely his elect who abide under his shadow.

Affirming even more so the guarding power of God's angelic beings, Scripture shows in multiple places that the strength of God's angels is unmatched. Other than God himself, no greater beings can offer such great protection to God's people like God's angelic army. These beings have fought and will continue to fight in some of the most significant battles in the universe.

There is a constant battle between good and evil that is going on behind the scenes in the spiritual realm, and it is God's angels who are on the front lines of this battle, fighting against the prince of the air and his demons, guarding those who are God's elect. To emphasize the comfort found under the shadow of the Almighty, Moses shows us in v. 11 that there is a plurality of angels God sends, not just one, to aid in our preservation. In 2 Kgs 6:15–17, a small glimpse is given of the numerous angels God dispatches to help his people in their preservation. When the King of Syria wages war against Israel, Elisha and his servant watch as the vast Syrian army approaches the border of Israel with their many chariots and horses and men. As Elisha watches, he does not begin to worry or fret because he knows God surrounds his people with an angelic army to protect them. However, his servant was very fearful of the situation. As Elisha's servant looked on in fear, he said to Elisha, "Alas, my master! How shall we do? And he answered, fear not: for they that be with us are more than they that be with them." After Elisha prays for God to open the eyes of the young man, he saw God's army of angelic beings surrounding them and the city as the Syrian army attempted to destroy them. God's army of angelic beings surrounded his two servants and his city as an army of Syrians attempted to destroy it, preserving them.

In Ps 91, Moses describes a common action of God's angels, namely their use in fighting for and guarding of God's people. In the last part of v. 11, Moses shows that the duty of God's angels is to keep his people in all their ways. The word for "keep" is the same word used when God tells Adam to "keep" the garden of Eden. It means "to preserve" or "to guard." The way this verb is written as an infinitive means that it modifies the main verb of God's charging or commanding his angels. In other words, Moses says that the heart of God's command to his angels is to "keep" or "guard" those abiding under his shadow. The old adage is true: God has guardian angels watching over his people. It is a wonderful comfort to know that God is not only keeping you under his pinions and wings, according to v. 4, but he even sends his strongest of creation to guard you and keep you in all your ways.

THE EXTENT OF OUR PRESERVATION (VV. 12–13)

How do God's angels keep his people? What does it look like for God's angels to keep his people? Moses provides answers to these questions in vv. 12–13. Moses says in v. 12, "They shall bear thee up in their hands, lest thou dash thy foot against a stone." These angels who abide under the shadow of the Almighty provide preventative care to you and me. Moses describes them in this verse as being more proactive than reactive in preserving God's people. Instead of waiting for something to happen to God's people or for one to fall on their own, these angels bear them up, or, more literally, carry them in the hollow of their hands. God's preventative care through his angels is one of God's greatest mercies. Through his keeping and restraining of them, God prevents those who abide under his shadow from falling into condemnation spiritually.

The imagery Moses uses in Ps 91 to describe God's preserving power is beautiful. Moses has already shown how God is like a mother bird who preserves her chicks under her wings, but God's angelic beings are also described as carrying God's people in the hollow of their hands as they make their way to heaven to be with him forever. There is no safer place to be than under the shadow of the Almighty, because those who are there are also being carried in the palms of God's angelic army. Spurgeon adds more to the imagery of God's angels carrying his own in the palms of their hands, saying, "As nurses carry little children, with careful love, so shall those glorious spirits bear up each individual believer."[2]

The use of the word "hand" in v. 12 as a place of security is not unusual but is seen all throughout Scripture in the same light. The hand of God is often described as a place of security for the believer. In many places in the Old Testament, because "God's good

---

2. Spurgeon, "Treasury of David, Psalm 91."

hand" was upon his people, they prospered and were preserved. Moses reminded God's people many times that God's strong hand had delivered them from the iron furnace of Egypt. In Exod 13:3, Moses says, "Remember this day, in which ye came out from Egypt, out of the house of bondage; for by strength of hand the Lord brought you out from this place: there shall no leavened bread be eaten." In Exod 13:9, he says again concerning God's hand of delivery, "For with a strong hand hath the Lord brought thee out of Egypt." Moses continues to remind God's people in the remainder of Exod 13 of God's preserving power through his strong hand. Jesus, being fully God, also references not only his Father's hand but his hand as well as the very thing that keeps and guards his sheep when he says in John 10:28–29, "And I give unto them eternal life; and they shall never perish, neither shall any man pluck them out of my hand. My Father, which gave them me, is greater than all; and no man is able to pluck them out of my Father's hand." Thus, according to Scripture, those who are God's people are kept in the Father's hand, in Jesus's hand, and also in the hands of God's angels; therefore, there is no safer place to be than under the shadow of the Almighty, where this preservation is found.

So what are his angels keeping those who abide under his shadow from? Moses says God's angels keep these from "dashing thy foot against a stone." Some commentators claim that Moses is trying to show that if God is willing to guard something as insignificant as a foot being injured, how much more will he be concerned about guarding the lives of his people? However, there seems to be more of a spiritual aspect to this verse than simply guarding one's body or foot. Sin in Scripture is often associated with stumbling or falling, so it seems that Moses is saying that God is so concerned about your spiritual preservation that he sends his angels to guard you from the smallest of trips and falls into sin, so it does not lead to greater sin.

Regarding God's preventative care in our stumbling, Charles Spurgeon says, "It is most desirable that we should not stumble, but as the way is rough, it is most gracious on the Lord's part to send his servants to bear us up above the loose pebbles. If we cannot have the way smoothed, it answers every purpose if we have angels to bear us up in their hands. Since the greatest ills may arise out of little accidents, it shows the wisdom of the Lord that from the smaller evils we are protected."[3] Paul, in his letter to the Galatians, reminds them of the dangers of sin and how just a little sin can fester into a life of sin, saying "a little leaven leaveneth the whole lump" (Gal 5:9). Thankfully, God, through many different means, including the use of his angels, keeps his people from succumbing to greater evils by bringing them to repentance of their more minor evils.

From the smallest of stones to the raging lion, the cobra, and the dragon, Moses shows us in v. 13 the extent of the dangers God protects his people from. From the smallest of spiritual threats, such as a small stone that may cause one to go deeper into sin, to the greatest of threats, such as a young lion who is a picture of Satan himself, who is the greatest of deceivers and will devour you by temptation to sin—God's preservation from these will not fail. Notice the three animals Moses describes: a lion, a serpent, and a dragon; each of these is used to represent Satan in Scripture. Moses is essentially saying that God protects and preserves those who abide under his shadow not only from themselves and their desire to sin but also from the Evil One. Moses alluded to the Evil One earlier when he promised that God would deliver those who abide under his shadow from the "snare of the fowler" (v. 3). As stated earlier, many commentators believe the "fowler" mentioned in v. 3 refers to Satan. Thankfully, through God's preservation, Moses says that those who abide under the shadow of the Almighty can tread on these enemies, including Satan. For those who abide under God's shadow, God will give you victory over the Evil One, allowing you to tread over him because of the salvation that God has given you in Christ.

---

3. Spurgeon, "Treasury of David, Psalm 91."

CONCLUSION

Although Moses may not have fully understood that his words in Ps 91 pointed toward a greater victory, namely the triumph believers have in Christ over their greatest enemies such as sin, death, and Satan, our preservation comes from being in Christ, who has defeated and destroyed not only sin, but also death, hell, and the grave. Because of him, we who are in Christ share in that victory. By bearing on the cross the sins of man, satisfying God's divine wrath, and destroying death on the cross, Christ has given victory and the means of preservation to those for whom he died. Therefore, whoever abides in Christ has conquered death, Satan, and sin. His victory is our victory; consequently, we do not have to worry about fighting a battle that we cannot win against sin and the devil because the battle is already won. We can have peace knowing that God has already defeated our greatest enemies in Christ. Thus, not one of them will ever be able to separate us from the love of God, which is in Christ Jesus our Lord (Rom 8:31–39). Since Christ paid for our sins with his blood, God the Father redeeming us with the blood of his only begotten son, surely God will not lose any of those in whom he has paid such a high cost for. Jesus promises that all that the Father has given him, he will raise all of them up in the last day (John 6:39–40).

God's preserving power for his people is found in Ps 91 and validated throughout Scripture. Not only does God personally keep those who are his in his hand, but his angels also are sent to keep his people in the hollows or palms of their hand. God will bring his elect to glory; he will bring them to their inheritance, and he will do so through his preserving power (1 Pet 1: 3–6). As the author and finisher of the believer's faith, God is the one who not only begins our faith but sustains our faith to the very end. It is God the Father who, through Christ, has begun a good work in his believers. Thus, it must be God the Father who will complete that good work (Phil 1:6). Like Moses, Paul confirms the preservation of God's people in that golden chain of salvation he mentions in Rom 8:30, saying, "Moreover whom he did predestinate, them he also called: and whom he called, them he also justified; and whom he justified, them he also glorified." So, for all whom God has saved, namely all who abide in him, Paul's statement in Rom 8:30 shows that these are guaranteed to be glorified. If everyone God has called will be glorified, then Paul's certainty in stating "whom he called, them he also glorified" (Rom 8:30) must rest on God's power to preserve his people; only God can provide such a guarantee. In this passage, Paul does not say that *some* of those called will be glorified, nor that they *might* be glorified, but that *all* in whom God has genuinely called will be justified, and all of these will be glorified.

In Rom 8:30, the verb "glorified" (*edoxasen*) is in the aorist tense, denoting a completed action. Writing the verb "glorified" in the aorist tense is interesting because the believer's glorification is still in the future. However, Paul speaks of it as if it has already been accomplished. Paul's use of the prophetic past or proleptic aorist of the verb for the word "glorified" emphasizes the assurance of God's promise. Even though the believer's glorification is the final stage of salvation, Paul's reference to it in the aorist tense emphasizes that those whom God has predestined, called, and justified will undoubtedly be glorified because it has already been written in God's story, which God has already written. There is no possibility of failure in God's redemptive work because there is no possibility of God's story changing—he has already written it from the beginning to the end (Isa 46: 8–11). Therefore, nothing will change the believer's status as one in whom, in the prophetic past, God has already written in his story as one who will be glorified. As seen in Paul's words in Rom 8:30, Moses's in Ps 91, and most of Scripture, the preservation of God's saints is rooted in God's faithfulness to bring those for whom he paid with his Son's blood to their final glory. Thus, the believer's assurance that they will one day be with God in heaven is rooted in God's faithfulness, not human effort. Therefore, no man can boast in himself, but only in God. God preserves his people through different means, namely those who abide under his shadow. Through the use of angels, through the prayers of his saints, and even by his hand, he keeps those who are his. Our glorification is guaranteed because it depends on God's sovereign preservation, not our strength. For those who abide under the shadow of the Almighty, you will be preserved from your physical enemies and your spiritual enemies, allowing you, through God's strength, to make it to your final glorification with God in heaven. May we all rest in this truth and be assured that God, who has begun good work in us, will complete it.

6

A Life Marked by Longevity
Psalm 91:14–16

INTRODUCTION

SINCE THE FALL OF humanity, as shown in Gen 2–3, the lives of humans have been cut short through disease, disasters, aging, and many other means of physical decay. Since death is inevitable, many have attempted and still do attempt to delay their deaths and add longevity to their lives. The pursuit of longevity has been and continues to be one of the world's most sought-after desires. People will give practically anything for a longer life, including money and time. Many have pursued longevity through various means: healthy eating, exercise, medication, and more. Businesses have capitalized on this desire, with the global anti-aging market projected to reach $274.5 billion by 2025, growing at 5.7 percent annually.[1] The United States spends $12.8 billion yearly on anti-aging products, with individuals investing $150–$200 annually in supplements.[2]

1. Grand View Research, "Anti-Aging Products."
2. Grand View Research, "Anti-Aging Products."

A Life Marked by Longevity

Despite these efforts, humans are still unable to reverse the aging process completely and add substantial longevity to their lives. However, the quest for longevity remains strong. Even though great effort has been taken to find the silver bullet to aging, folks have not been able to reverse the aging process, proving their efforts futile, to say the least. Even with extensive research on anti-aging and how to promote it in humans, the answer to what truly brings longevity is unclear. If only folks would look to Scripture, specifically Ps 91, the quest for longevity would be over. Many places in Scripture point to the source of our longevity, namely God, as the only one who sustains life and, therefore, provides longevity if he desires to do so. Scriptures like Ps 91 are packed full of promises and works of God that provide longevity to those who simply abide under his shadow.

Therefore, where can humanity find longevity of life? According to Ps 91, longevity of life is exclusive to those who continually abide in Yahweh (v. 1a) because only these will find themselves living under the shadow of Yahweh, with all of its benefits. Thomas Watson once said, "Long life is a mercy to a saint; it is a blessing to have time to serve God, and to get acquaintance with him."[3] Psalm 91 confirms Watson's statement by showing its readers that God's mercy provides longevity of life to those who abide under his shadow. Psalm 91:14–16 reminds us that longevity, a universal human aspiration, is a divine gift that God himself promises to those who abide under his shadow.

The entirety of Ps 91 crescendos in these latter verses when the speaker changes from Moses to God. In vv. 14–16, God speaks, confirming and affirming all that Moses has said concerning life under the shadow of the Almighty. In his discourse, Yahweh in these latter verses sums up all Moses has said thus far regarding this life under the shadow of the Almighty as a life marked by longevity and complete satisfaction. From vv. 1–13, Moses provides promises of the works of God that, when put together, bring about longevity to those who abide under his shadow. From resting or lodging under God's shadow to being partakers of his

---

3. Watson, *Great Gain*, 136.

deliverance and protection, Moses shows that God provides everything needed to preserve and sustain the life of those who abide under his shadow. Therefore, in a triumphant conclusion to Ps 91, God himself speaks, bringing all of what Moses has said so far to its culmination, saying in v. 16, "With long life I will satisfy him, and shew him my salvation." The ultimate benefit of abiding under Yahweh's shadow is given by Yahweh himself in this verse. Everything Moses has promised so far regarding life under the shadow of the Almighty, when put together, brings about the longevity and satisfaction that Yahweh promises in v. 16. By bringing all of what Moses has said together in this one climax of a promise, it is as if God stamps his seal of approval onto what Moses has shown us during his tour through a life under the shadow of the Almighty.

In these last few verses, as God speaks, he confirms Moses's promises concerning him and expands on what he will do for those who abide under his shadow. God promises, as Moses does, that he will provide deliverance, but he expands on that promise by saying that he will answer those who abide under his shadow when they cry out for deliverance, while at the same time bringing honor to them (v. 15). God expands on all his promises in the last verse of this psalm, showing that all of his works of deliverance and protection lead to his ultimate work—bringing satisfaction to those who abide under his shadow—by giving them ultimately longevity of life: eternal life.

If Ps 91 has taught us anything, it is that one need not think twice about whether they should abide under the shadow of the Almighty, because life under the shadow of the Almighty is a life of blessing and, ultimately, fulfillment, a life that is both satisfied and honored in the Lord. As the reader comes to the end of his tour under the shadow of the Almighty in these last few verses, he hears from the One whose shadow provides all of these special blessings that Moses has spoken of so far: God himself, who speaks to us in the last part of this tour under the shadow of the Almighty. The Most High, the Almighty, as v. 1 calls him, the one who is called a place of refuge and fortress according to v. 2, begins to speak directly to the readers of Ps 91, showing that these promises will come to pass because they have been confirmed by God himself, who brings all that he wishes to pass (Isa 46:8–11).

In these last few verses, God offers many promises that are extensions of what Moses has already promised, ultimately leading to the greatest promise of the entire psalm, namely that for those who abide under the shadow of the Almighty, Yahweh himself will provide satisfaction through long life and his salvation. Therefore, if you desire long or eternal life, you must abide with Yahweh continually under his shadow. Let us look, then, at these promises that God himself gives to those who abide under his shadow at the end of this psalm, and let us take comfort in knowing that we as believers, through God's grace, have the option to abide under his wonderful shadow and receive all of these special promises.

PROMISE OF DELIVERANCE (V. 14)

Throughout vv. 1–13 of Ps 91, Moses is the speaker, providing promise after promise of what one will find while abiding under the shadow of the Almighty. Drawing from his experience in the exodus from Egypt to the promised land, Moses gives his readers a glimpse of the benefits they will find if they abide under the shadow of the Almighty by providing a personal testimony of what he saw while abiding there. Moses in his journey from Egypt through the Red Sea and into the wilderness had witnessed firsthand God's rest, God's deliverance, and God's protection and preservation, all of which he promises others will experience if only, according to v. 1, they continually abide in the "secret place of the Most High." Moses demonstrates that only those who continually abide with God will find themselves under the shadow of the Almighty and experience the same benefits and promises he received during his exodus journey. All the promises Moses presents in the first part of Ps 91—rest, deliverance, and protection for those who continually abide with Yahweh—are further validated at the end of the psalm when God himself speaks. This divine declaration affirms and confirms the claims Moses has already made about life under God's shadow in the preceding verses. No other could provide greater credibility to what Moses has said than God himself.

At the beginning of v. 14, Yahweh begins to list promises of what he will provide to those under his shadow. Before doing so, however, he, like Moses, provides a conditional statement, showing that only certain ones will be able to obtain the promises he is about to give. Confirming the conditionality that Moses gives back in v. 1, namely that only those "who abide in the secret places of the Most High" will be those who experience all the benefits that life offers under the shadow of the Almighty, God also affirms in v. 14 that it will be only those who have "set their love upon" him who will be the ones who will experience the promises mentioned in vv. 14–16. If this psalm has made one thing clear so far, it is that not all will experience the benefits a life under the shadow of the Almighty offers. Moses shows the exclusiveness of those who will find themselves under the shadow of the Almighty by stating in v. 1 that it will be only those who are "abiding in the secret places of the Most High." Moses doubles down in v. 9, showing that life under the shadow of the Almighty and its benefits are conditional in that only those who "hast made the LORD, which is my refuge, even the most High, thy habitation," will obtain these benefits. Both vv. 1 and 9 essentially expand on one another, showing that only those who abide continually with Yahweh (v. 1) are those who have made him their dwelling place (v. 9). To show that life under the shadow of the Almighty is conditional based on specific criteria, Moses begins v. 9 with a causal conjunction that can be translated as "for" or "because," showing that it is "because" one has done this that they will experience what Moses has just promised. Moses is saying to his readers that the reason you will experience the precious promises given in the previous verses regarding life under the shadow of the Almighty is "because you have made the Lord, who is my refuge, even the Most High, your dwelling place" (v. 9; my translation). Similarly, Yahweh starts his list of promises directed to those who abide under his shadow with a causal conjunction in v. 14, emphasizing the condition that one must meet to receive these promises rather than the promises themselves. By starting off his discourse the same way, it is as if God is saying Moses is right concerning the exclusiveness of those who experience blessings under his shadow; those blessings will be only for the one Yahweh says "hath set his love upon me" (v. 14).

The words "set his love" stems from two Hebrew words, one being a preposition and one being a perfect verb. The Hebrew preposition that comes before the verb "love" means "to set in place" or "strictly in a particular place"; thus, when attached to the verb "love," it can be translated as a "set love," as most English translations render it. In other words, the promises that Moses gives concerning those who abide under the shadow of the Almighty, which are further solidified by the promises that Yahweh is about to give in vv. 14–16, are exclusive to those who have "set" or "established" their love upon Yahweh. As a perfect verb, this love is a settled love; it is an established love, not a love yet to be determined but a love settled on Yahweh. Thus, this psalm ends the way it begins, with a conditional statement followed by a set of promises.

After giving the conditionality of his promises, Yahweh begins to confirm and validate the promises Moses has given in the previous verses while also expanding upon them. From Moses's promise that God will deliver those who abide under his shadow (v. 3), God confirms Moses's promise by saying in v. 14 that "because he hath set his love upon me, therefore I will deliver him." Moses provides meat to God's claim of deliverance back in v. 3, showing us how and what God will deliver us from, saying, "Surely he shall deliver thee from the snare of the fowler, and from the noisome pestilence." In v. 4, God promised to provide this deliverance by hiding those who abide under his shadow under his pinions or wings. Much like Moses, God does not leave questions about whether or not those who abide under his shadow will experience deliverance; he promises this deliverance. Like Moses, Yahweh shows that the promises he is about to make are guaranteed and not volatile. When giving his promises, God does not say that he "might" deliver or that he "may" deliver, but as a God whose promises will all come to pass, he says for those who "set their love" on him, he will deliver them. Just as Moses validates at the beginning of this psalm that God delivers those who are his, and as God himself validates his delivery of his people at the end of this psalm, the entirety of Scripture validates God's promises, specifically of deliverance for those who abide under his shadow.

David, a man after God's own heart who set his love on Yahweh, confesses many times that God has delivered him repeatedly and will continue to do so. Before David begins his testimony about how God delivered him from some of the most trying times and enemies of his life, David makes sure to confirm that he has met the condition that Yahweh has set for those he will deliver, namely the setting of one's love upon Yahweh. David shows he has first met Yahweh's condition of setting his love upon him in v. 1 of Ps 18, saying, "I love you, O LORD, my strength" (ESV). After David confirms his love for Yawheh, he then gives testimony of Yahweh's deliverance in his life, showing that Yahweh upholds his end of the deal when one sets their love upon him. After proclaiming his love for Yahweh, David, in the beginning of Ps 18, describes the utter terror he faced because of those who desired him dead, saying in vv. 4–5, "The sorrows of death compassed me, and the floods of ungodly men made me afraid. The sorrows of hell compassed me about: the snares of death prevented me." After describing the desperate situation that he was in, David then shows in v. 6 that he called upon the One he loves, Yahweh, saying, "In my distress I called upon the LORD, and cried unto my God: he heard my voice out of his temple, and my cry came before him, even into his ears." David affirms that Yahweh heard his cries—the cries of the one who set his love upon him—which adds validity to Yahweh's claim in Ps 91:15, in which he promises that to the one who calls upon him that "I will answer him."

David then gives testimony in the remainder of Ps 18 of Yahweh, the One in whom David has set his love upon, coming to rescue him. Just as Yahweh promises in Ps 91:15 that not only will he hear the one who has set their love upon him, but he "will be with him in trouble" and "deliver him," David shows that Yahweh does just that when he calls upon him. Yahweh hears David, who loves him, and quickly comes to his aid. In Ps 18:10, David says, regarding Yahweh's quick response to his deliverance, "And he rode upon a cherub, and did fly: yea, he did fly upon the wings of the wind," until finally David's cries for deliverance are answered. David notes this in v. 17, saying "He delivered me from my strong enemy, and from them which hated me: for they were too strong for me."

Many other psalms show Yahweh's deliverance to those who set their love upon him. In Ps 23, David again gives testimony of Yahweh's delivering power, this time from one of man's greatest enemies: death. David confesses in Ps 23:4 of Yahweh's deliverance of him from the darkest of valleys that David had tread so far, saying, "Yea, though I walk through the valley of the shadow of death, I will fear no evil: for thou art with me; thy rod and thy staff they comfort me." David confirms in Ps 23 that God's deliverance is not limited in any way but is powerful enough to deliver even from the grips of death and the darkest of life's valleys. Even more profound is Yahweh's deliverance of humankind from their sins. In Ps 86:13, the psalmist demonstrates Yahweh's deliverance from sin and judgment, saying, "For great is thy mercy toward me: and thou hast delivered my soul from the lowest hell."

The greatest deliverance a man or a woman will ever experience is their deliverance from sin, thus their deliverance from the judgment of Yahweh. Many places in the New Testament confirm that God only delivers from their sins those who have set their love upon him. Having faith in Christ alone is the greatest evidence of one's set love upon God, and it is this faith in Christ alone that provides the greatest deliverance man will ever experience, namely his deliverance from sin and the wrath of God. Jesus describes this set love that is required to be delivered from sin in Matt 16:24, this faith that sets a man free, when he says to be saved one must "deny himself, and take up his cross, and follow me." A person shows his set love on Yahweh by denying himself, taking up his cross, and following Yahweh with all of his being, which is what Jesus called all those who will follow him to do so that they may inherit eternal life.

THE MECHANICS OF HIS DELIVERANCE (VV. 14B–16)

Using synthetic parallelism, the psalmist builds upon the previous clauses presented at the beginning of v. 14, first giving us the promise of deliverance and then explaining what that deliverance will look like. Yahweh says, "I will deliver him"; then he describes how, saying, "I will set him on high, because he hath known my name." What is interesting is that v. 14 is chiastic in structure. At the beginning and the end of v. 14 is a causal conjunction, with the promise of deliverance tucked away in the middle. In other words, God says, "Because he hath set his love upon me," and "because he hath known my name," "therefore will I deliver him" by setting the believer on high. Yahweh's action of setting one on high is a picture of placing one in a high place out of the reach of their enemies. Like a mountain goat strides the highest parts of the mountain to avoid contact with the enemy, God delivers his people as such by setting them in high places so that they are out of the enemy's reach. The terminology of being "set on high" or "in high places" is seen in other psalms, particularly the psalms of David. David knew all too well what it was like to be on the run from the enemy continually. Often finding himself in a cave or some hideaway, God ensured David was hidden from his enemies, protecting his appointed king from destruction.

Not only did David in the early sections of Ps 18 state his love for God and God's rapid response in delivering him, but throughout the remainder of the same psalm, David describes what God's deliverance looks like. One way David describes Yahweh's deliverance of him is that Yahweh places David in a high place away from his enemies. In Ps 18:33, David says that God places him in a high place: "He maketh my feet like hinds' feet, and setteth me upon my high places." David thus confirms God's delivering habits of setting those who love him on high or in high places. In other words, God places us in a position where the enemy cannot destroy or harm us. The phrases "high" or "high places" often refer to places where

God places those he is protecting, hiding them away from their enemies.

The place of security that God provides is described in many ways throughout Scripture. Not only do Yahweh and David describe this place of security as a "high place," but Moses describes it earlier in v. 4 as being covered by God's feathers or pinions. Moses then alludes to the place of security that God provides as being in the palms of the angels' hands in v. 12. In general, those who abide under the shadow of the Almighty will find themselves in a place of security, just as both Moses and David experienced. In the New Testament, this place of security and deliverance is also described as tucked away in someone's hand, namely the hand of Christ and God the Father. Jesus in John 10:27–30 promises that those who are his sheep will experience security and provision inside the hands of both him and the Father, saying, "My sheep hear my voice, and I know them, and they follow me: And I give unto them eternal life; and they shall never perish, neither shall any man pluck them out of my hand. My Father, which gave them me, is greater than all; and no man is able to pluck them out of my Father's hand. I and my Father are one." Thus, the scope of Scripture confirms not only Yahweh's promise of deliverance to those who love him but also the many ways in which Yahweh delivers his people.

Promise to Listen, to Deliver, and to Honor (v. 15)

Verse 15 of Ps 91 confirms that those who abide under the shadow of the Almighty can be sure that God will hear them when they call upon him. God, still speaking in v. 15, promises that he will not only hear those who call out to him but also answer those who call upon him, saying, "He shall call upon me, and I will answer him." The third-person singular pronoun "he" refers to the "he" in v. 14, namely the one who has set their love upon Yahweh. God is saying it will only be the one who has set his love upon him that God will deliver and answer when he calls. God's promise to answer those believers who call upon him further extends his promise of deliverance. In other words, if one calls upon him for anything, especially for deliverance, God will make good on his promise and provide that deliverance to those who love him. Therefore, those who abide in the shadow of the Almighty never have to worry if God will hear their prayers, because Yahweh promises in v. 15 not only that he will hear them, but he will also answer them.

After promising to answer those who call upon him, Yahweh begins to give a series of promises that expand and expound upon the promises that Moses has already detailed throughout Ps 91 concerning Yahweh's deliverance. In rapid fire, God begins to show the extent of his answering to those who call out for his deliverance. In his answering those who have cried out for deliverance, God promises to first be with that one who has called out to him in their times of distress or trouble (v. 15b). For those abiding under the shadow of the Almighty, you can be sure that God will be with you in your times of trouble whenever you cry out to him. Yahweh's promise to be with those who call upon him in their times of trouble is one of the greatest promises in Scripture, and it should offer comfort to all who abide under his shadow. This promise reveals not only the delivering power of God but the intimacy of God with those who love him. In this promise, Yahweh shows himself to be a personal God who not only sends his angels to deliver those who are his but also to be a God who personally takes part in their deliverance by abiding with them during their times of trouble. The Hebrew shows the intimacy of Yahweh towards his people in v. 15. The first-person singular imperfect form of the verb *hayah*, or "to be," is translated here in v. 15 as "I will be." The imperfect tense of this verb conveys a continuous or future action, meaning Yahweh is making a promise that he will continually be with those who abide under his shadow in their times of trouble. Interestingly, *ehyeh* is the same root as God's self-revelation seen in Exod 3:14, in which God says, "I am who I am," or *Ehyeh Asher Ehyeh*, reinforcing that the God of Israel is the one who abides with his people in their times of trouble. The next Hebrew word in this verse is a preposition combined with the third-person singular suffix forming the word *'immō*, or "with him," expressing that Yahweh will personally be "with him," or the one who loves him, in their times of trouble. Many other Scriptures attest to Yahweh's intimacy with his people, being with them in their times of need.

Psalm 46 is another famous psalm providing testimony to God's delivering presence with his people during times of trouble, saying from the outset, "God is our refuge and strength, a very present help in trouble." Moses understood wholeheartedly that God will be present with his people in their distress. Thus, Moses asks the Israelites a question in Deut 4:7, reminding them of how blessed they are to worship a God that stayed so near them, especially in their times of trouble. Moses poses this question to the Israelites as a reminder of God's presence with them in their times of trouble: "For what nation is there so great, who hath God so nigh unto them, as the LORD our God is in all things that we call upon him for?" In other words, Moses is asking the Israelites rhetorically, "What other nation has experienced such closeness with God, especially during times of trouble, like you have, Israel?" The clear answer is that no other nation has been so blessed. Thus, Israel is blessed because they have a God that sticks so close to them, even during times of great peril. Psalm 9 is yet another psalm that describes the closeness of God to those who are his in their times of trouble, saying in v. 9, "The LORD also will be a refuge for the oppressed, a refuge in times of trouble." Scripture is clear that Yahweh is close to those who are his in their times of trouble, especially those who abide under his shadow. In times of great trouble, the presence of Yahweh is often felt the most, especially by those who abide under his shadow.

In the next portion of Ps 91:15, Yahweh continues doubling down on his promise to deliver the one who abides under his shadow, namely the one who has set his love upon him, by saying again at the end of v. 15, "I will deliver him," then adding "and honour him." Yahweh promises that his deliverance will also be married with honoring those who have called upon him, essentially giving them more than they asked of him. Giving his people more than they asked for is not unusual for God when he blesses those who are his. God's overabundance in blessing his people is seen in Eph 3:20–21, where Paul says in his doxology, "Now unto him that is able to do exceeding abundantly above all that we ask or think, according to the power that worketh in us, Unto him be glory in the church by Christ Jesus throughout all ages, world without end. Amen." The "him" Paul refers to in this passage is Yahweh God, who is able to and often does give more to those who call upon him than they asked for. Here in Ps 91:15, God validates his abundant giving by not only promising to deliver those who call upon him but also promising to honor them as well. The words "and honor him" can also be translated as "and bring him to honor." Thus, for those who abide under the shadow of the Almighty, God will deliver you and bring you from dishonor to a state of honor, exalting you from your lowly state. In other words, God exalts all those who "set their love" upon him, namely those who abide under his shadow.

The concept of God exalting the lowly is seen throughout Scripture. Other psalms confirm God's exaltation of those who are lowly and are in times of trouble. In Ps 71:21, the psalmist says concerning Yahweh's exaltation of him, "Thou shalt increase my greatness, and comfort me on every side." In Ps 113:7-8, the psalmist says concerning Yahweh's power in exalting those who are lowly, "He raiseth up the poor out of the dust, and lifteth the needy out of the dunghill; That he may set him with princes, even princes of his people." In Ps 113:7, the extent of Yahweh's exaltation of his people is seen when Yahweh takes one who is poor and in an ash heap or dunghill and, through his power, lifts them to the opposite extreme of poverty, namely, to be in a position next to princes and kings. God's exaltation of his people is not a light matter but very significant: to exalt dead sinners who are barred from heaven to a place of being a joint heir with Christ, God sent his Son to die for the sins of the many, to provide a way for those who live under his shadow be exalted.

The extreme exaltation of God's people in their salvation is seen in Jesus's words in the Sermon on the Mount. Jesus, in his promise statements presented in the Beatitudes, shows the lowly being exalted when he says, "Happy are the poor in spirit because theirs is the kingdom of God" (my translation). Jesus continues his beatific statements by claiming that it will be "the meek who will inherit the earth," and so on, showing this great exaltation of those the world considers to be the lowliest of people. While the world exalts those who have some prominence already, God in his kingdom economy exalts those whom the world has cast off, namely the poor and the broken. It will be these who will eventually inherit the earth in their exaltation. So it is that we see repeatedly that God will bring honor to those who set their love upon him by exalting them from their lowly state.

PROMISE OF LONG LIFE (V. 16)

Psalm 91:16 provides the climax of the entire psalm, giving the ultimate benefit of abiding under the shadow of the Almighty, namely that those who do so will experience satisfaction through the longevity of life. Those who abide under the shadow of the Almighty will experience longevity of life, and rightfully so, considering what Moses and God have promised so far. Rest, deliverance, protection, lack of fear, preservation, and many other benefits of living under the shadow of the Almighty all work in tandem to provide longevity to those who abide under the Almighty's shadow. In the final verses of this psalm, one of the greatest promises ever given to those who love God is given by God himself, saying, "With long life I will satisfy him, and shew him my salvation." If anyone desires long life, a life of true satisfaction and *shalom* (peace) that can only stem from a covenantal relationship with Yahweh, then they must find themselves under the shadow of the Almighty. No other God can provide length of life but this God, who is the Most High and the Almighty (v. 1). Yahweh personally confirms that he alone has the power to provide longevity, and he will do so only for those who find themselves under his shadow. The one who is the genesis of all life is the only one who can make such a promise, which is given here at the end of Ps 91. No created thing can promise longevity of life—only the Uncreated One, the One who has always been, Yahweh God, who is self-existent alone, who has the power to give and sustain life. Scripture begins with Yahweh's power over life and ends with Yahweh's power over life. The book of Genesis opens with Yahweh's creation of order and life, while the book of Revelation closes with Yahweh's creation of a new order and life in the new heavens and earth. Yahweh alone has the power to give life and to take it away (1 Sam 2:6; John 10:18).

The longevity of life that God promises in v. 16 correlates with God's deliverance, which God and Moses have promised throughout this psalm to those who abide under his shadow. The entirety of Ps 91 explains how God provides longevity to those who abide under his shadow. Longevity of life is born through God's deliverance of his people from the "snare of the fowler, and from the noisome pestilence," according to v. 3. Longevity of life also stems from God tucking in close to him under his wing those who abide under his shadow, acting as a place of refuge to these, according to v. 4. The remainder of the psalm shows that this longevity of life comes through God striking down the enemies of those who abide under his shadow. Verses 5–10 expound upon God's delivering his people from their enemies, promising not only a life absent of fear but longevity of life. According to these verses, Yahweh delivers his people from the "terror by night," the "arrow that flieth by day," and even the "pestilence that walketh in darkness," along with the "destruction that wasteth at noonday" (v. 5–6). Verses 7–8 show that longevity of life comes to those who are able to watch God destroy their enemies one by one, saying, "A thousand shall fall at thy side, and ten thousand at thy right hand; but it shall not come nigh thee. Only with thine eyes shalt thou behold and see the reward of the wicked." Moses then summarizes God's deliverance—and the exclusivity of his deliverance to only those who make him their God—saying in vv. 9–10, "Because thou hast made the LORD, which is my refuge, even the most High, thy habitation; There shall no evil befall thee, neither shall any plague come nigh thy dwelling." To add more validity and meat to how God brings longevity to those who abide under his shadow, Moses continues in vv. 11–13 by noting that God even dispatches his angels to keep watch over those who are his. In vv. 11–12, Moses promises that God will "give his angels charge over thee, to keep thee in all thy

A Life Marked by Longevity

ways. They shall bear thee up in their hands, lest thou dash thy foot against a stone."

This psalm then concludes by giving us God's very own words, showing how he plans to bring longevity to those who have set their love upon him. God provides longevity through his deliverance, as mentioned in v. 14; through his answering of prayer, as mentioned in v. 15; and through bringing those in whom he delivers honor, as mentioned at the end of v. 15. Psalm 91 shows that Yahweh is the giver of life and the keeper and sustainer of all life, especially those who abide under his shadow.

Verse 16 acts as a crescendo for Ps 91, showing that all the works of God in the life of those who dwell in his shadow lead up to his giving of longevity of life. In other words, those who dwell under the shadow of the Almighty will find that God will work in their lives in such a way that they will have years added to their life and life added to their years. God closes this psalm by saying that in his giving of long life to those who abide in his shadow, he will not only provide satisfaction to them but also reveal his salvation to them. God's salvation is exclusive to those who abide under his shadow; it is only under his shadow that his salvation is seen and experienced. There is no question that one can find true salvation and longevity if they abide under the shadow of the Almighty. So what does finding salvation look like under the shadow of the Almighty?

CONCLUSION

For the believer, namely those who have placed their faith in Christ alone, those who have repented and who believe the gospel, only these will find themselves under the shadow of the Almighty, where such a great salvation will mark their lives. Longevity and deliverance are seen only by those in Christ, not simply longevity of this life but longevity that is marked by eternal life. Those who abide in Christ are those who abide under the shadow of the Almighty. Those in Christ will be the only ones to experience true longevity of life, a life that will never end, because Christ has granted them eternal life for believing in him. The benefits that Moses and Yahweh speak of regarding those under the shadow of the Almighty are but a small shadow of the benefits one will find when they abide in Christ.

Those abiding in Christ will find the ultimate rest, deliverance, protection, preservation, and so on that this psalm has described. Those in Christ will be kept from the Evil One, the snare of the fowler, and so on. Only those in Christ will no longer live with fear because Christ has already conquered their greatest enemies, enemies far greater than physical enemies, such as death, hell, the grave, sin, and Satan. Christ conquered these enemies once and for all when he died on the cross and was raised again three days later. Through his death and resurrection, Christ conquered all of humankind's greatest enemies, allowing only those in him to be conquerors over these great enemies. Therefore, only those who continually abide with Christ, taking up their cross, denying themselves, and following him will experience all of these promises that Moses and Yahweh have detailed in Ps 91 on a much grander scale. Interestingly, just as Yahweh promises longevity of life at the end of this psalm, Jesus does the same to those who follow him, namely because Jesus is Yahweh. As God the Son, Jesus provides longevity of life and satisfaction to those who abide in him; he is the one who gives eternal life to his sheep, promising that they will never perish.

Therefore, if you desire a life absent of fear, a life that is marked by true peace, a life absent of your enemies, and a life that will never end but continue into eternity, then you must abide in Christ, as only those who abide in Christ will be under his shadow and will be given eternal life. In God's grace, Moses has given us a taste of what life looks like for those who abide under the shadow of the Almighty, namely those now who abide in Christ. Moses has shown us that there is no sweeter place to be than under the shadow of the God who is sovereign over all things, the God who is sovereign ever over your life. My encouragement to you is that if you are seeking peace and freedom from anxiety and the perils that this fallen world offers, then abide in Christ, and there you will find yourself under the shadow of the Almighty.

Bibliography

"Anti-Aging Products Market Size, Share & Trends Analysis Report By Product (Facial Cream & Lotion, Eye Cream & Lotion), By Distribution Channel (Hypermarket & Supermarket, Specialty Store), And Segment Forecasts, 2021–2028." Grand View Research. https://www.grandviewresearch.com/industry-analysis/anti-aging-products-market.

Brooks, Thomas. *Heaven on Earth: A Treatise on Christian Assurance*. Edinburgh: Banner of Truth, 1961.

Brown, Francis, et al. *The Brown-Driver-Briggs Hebrew and English Lexicon*. Peabody, MA: Hendrickson, 1971.

———. *The Brown-Driver-Briggs Hebrew and English Lexicon: With an Appendix Containing the Biblical Aramaic: Coded with the Numbering System from Strong's Exhaustive Concordance of the Bible*. Peabody, MA: Hendrickson, 2015.

Freeman, James M. *Manners and Customs of the Bible*. Plainfield, NJ: Logos, 1972.

Gaebelein, Frank E., ed. *Psalms, Proverbs, Ecclesiastes, Song of Songs*. Vol. 5 of *Expositor's Bible Commentary*. Grand Rapids: Zondervan, 1991.

Gill, John. *Exposition of the Old Testament*. Vol. 4. London: Baptist Standard Bearer, 1989.

Henry, Matthew. *Matthew Henry's Exposition of the Old and New Testaments*. Vol. 1. Grand Rapids: Hendrickson, 1991.

Liddell, Henry G., et al. *A Greek-English Lexicon*. Oxford: Clarendon, 1996.

Longman III, Tremper, et al. *Psalms*. Vol. 5 of *The Expositor's Bible Commentary*. Grand Rapids: Zondervan, 1991.

Luther, Martin. "A Mighty Fortress Is Our God." *The Baptist Hymnal*, 216. Nashville: LifeWay Worship, 2008.

Owen, John. *Temptation and Sin*. Vol. 6 of *The Works of John Owen*. Edited by William H. Goold. Edinburgh: Banner of Truth, 1965.

Penner, Ken. *The Lexham English Septuagint*. 2nd ed. Bellingham, WA: Lexham, 2020.

Sarna, Nahum M. *On the Book of Psalms: Exploring the Prayers of Ancient Israel*. New York: Schocken, 1993.

Bibliography

Spurgeon, Charles H. *The Salt-Cellars: Being a Collection of Proverbs Together with Homely Notes Thereon.* Vol. 1. London: Passmore and Alabaster, 1889.
———. *The Treasury of David.* Vol. 2. Peabody, MA: Hendrickson, 1990.
———. *The Treasury of David.* Vol. 3. London: Passmore and Alabaster, 1886.
———. "The Treasury of David: Psalm 91." Blue Letter Bible. https://www.blueletterbible.org/Comm/spurgeon_charles/tod/ps091.cfm.
Watson, Thomas. *A Body of Divinity.* London: Thomas Tegg, 1832.
———. *A Divine Cordial.* Edinburgh: Banner of Truth, 1981.
———. *The Great Gain of Godliness.* Edinburgh: Banner of Truth, 1971.

www.ingramcontent.com/pod-product-compliance
Lightning Source LLC
Chambersburg PA
CBHW071730090426
42738CB00011B/2439